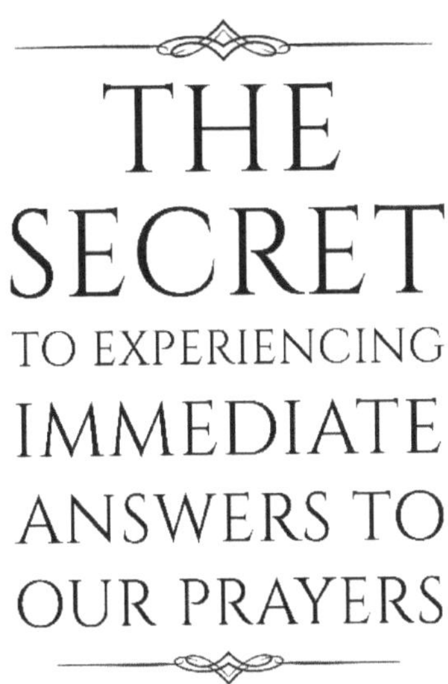

THE SECRET TO EXPERIENCING IMMEDIATE ANSWERS TO OUR PRAYERS

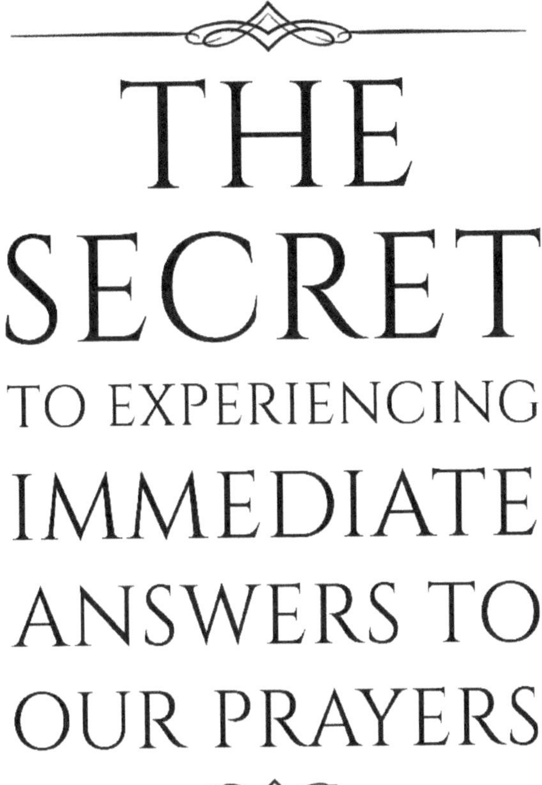

THE SECRET TO EXPERIENCING IMMEDIATE ANSWERS TO OUR PRAYERS

The Divine Revelation that Transforms
Cries of the Heart into Exploits

BOVIC TSHIAMALA

This English edition is a translation of the original French work:

"Le Secret pour Vivre l'Exaucement Immédiat de Nos Prières" © 2026 by Bovic Tshiamala.

Translation © 2026 by the author.

Published in Grapevine, Texas, by the author.

First English Edition

ISBN 978-1-971121-00-0 (eBook)
ISBN 978-1-971121-01-7 (paperback)
ISBN 978-1-971121-02-4 (hardcover)

Library of Congress Cataloging-in-Publication Data

Library of Congress Control Number: 2026900094

Printed in the United States of America

We dedicate this book to God, our Creator and Father of our Lord Jesus Christ, who, in His sovereign grace, has revealed to us the hidden mysteries that make the very act of answered prayer possible—mysteries established since the beginning, yet never heard by human ears.

To Him be glory, honor, power, and dominion, forever and ever.

Amen!

CONTENTS

THE TIMELESS TRUTH

"In God we will do mighty deeds" (Psalm 60:12 EHV).

This biblical affirmation is neither a mere slogan nor a truth frozen in the era of biblical accounts. Nor is it a formula intended to seduce the weak and destitute, as the devil would have us believe. On the contrary, it is a timeless truth that we too can experience in the various spheres of our lives—despite our limitations—for the prophet Moses, Joshua the son of Nun, King David, the prophet Elijah, the prophet Elisha, the apostle Peter, the apostle Paul, and many others who experienced it were human beings of the same nature as we are.

Let us not allow our past failures, difficult circumstances, or the apparent lack of answers to our prayers to imprison us in doubt and despair.

With God, we too can:

- Pray or declare, and witness miracles, wonders, healings, and more, taking place in our lives or the lives of those around us, just as experienced by:
    - The prophet Elijah (1 Kings 18:36–38)
    - The apostle Peter (Acts 3:1–8)
    - The apostle Paul (Acts 14:8–10)
- Command the elements of nature and see them obey, as Joshua the son of Nun did in the battle when the sun and moon stood still (Joshua 10:12–14)
- Face adversaries much stronger than we are and triumph, as King David did against Goliath (1 Samuel 17:41–51)

We can do it—and even more than these biblical figures did—for there is a secret that makes it possible. An ancient secret, hidden since the beginning, yet known to very few.

Today, we are the most blessed, for in His infinite benevolence, the Most High has revealed this secret to us in its entirety. He has also allowed us to share it for the edification of those who believe in His existence and in His promise to reward those who seek Him fervently.

This secret is eight spiritual dimensions, which, when attained, stimulate immediate answers to all our prayers.

To fully reveal these eight spiritual dimensions, we will unveil the hidden mysteries of the prayer-answering process, more precisely those of the two stages that comprise it: prayer and the answering of prayer. We will present them as they have been revealed to us, for within these mysteries lie the eight spiritual dimensions that stimulate immediate answers to all our prayers.

It is in this prophetic dimension—guided by the Most High and illuminated by His revealing light—that we will now enter into the heart of this revelation, which is not a mere doctrinal exposition, but access to an ancient spiritual path, traced and marked out by the Most High Himself for those who desire to see their prayers bear fruit without delay.

Chapter 1

PRAYER

In its first definition, prayer is the act of addressing God.

It can be practiced standing, sitting, kneeling, prostrating, or lying on the ground, alone or in community, aloud or in silence, in joy or in tears, in any place, at any time, and in many other ways, as long as these ways remain in accordance with God's laws and principles.

Its main function is to enable us to present our thoughts, feelings, requests, and gratitude to God, as the Holy Scriptures exhort us through these inspired words:

> "Do not be anxious about anything, but in every situation, by prayer and petition, with thanksgiving, present your requests to God" (Philippians 4:6).

In its second definition, prayer is a divine institution entrusted with the spiritual transmission of words—whether spoken aloud or in silence—from the creature to God.

As for its origin, prayer was established by God at the beginning of creation, even before the existence of the first creature capable of addressing Him.

On an operational level, prayer manages spiritual communication in a unidirectional manner: from the creature (sender) to God (receiver), not the other way around.

This is explained by the fact that the Most High uses other means to respond to prayers that reach His ears—means that we will unveil in the next chapter.

Like every divine institution, prayer is governed by a fundamental principle: every creature who desires to be heard by God must first approach His throne.

This is why the Holy Scriptures exhort us:

> "Let us then approach God's throne of grace with confidence, so that we may receive mercy and find grace to help us in our time of need" (Hebrews 4:16).

God established prayer according to this principle, for it contains mysteries that are crucial for prayer to be heard.

These mysteries lie in the approach to the throne of God, which enables us to attain a spiritual state that allows prayer to operate within us without restriction as to what it transmits.

What is this spiritual state that allows prayer, as a divine institution, to operate within us without restriction as to what it transmits?

How can we attain it?

To answer these questions, let us unveil the mysteries surrounding the very act of approaching the throne of God, for that is where the true dynamic of prayer begins.

THE APPROACH TO THE THRONE OF GOD

Where does it take place?

The approach to the throne of God—without which our act of addressing God would be reduced to a mere monologue—takes place in our spirit, for it is the only part of us that can approach the throne of God and communicate with Him.

It is this invisible yet real reality that the Lord Jesus Christ meant to express through the phrase "worship in spirit," when He declared with authority and clarity:

> "God is spirit, and those who worship him must worship in spirit and in truth" (John 4:24 EHV).

How is it done?

The approach to the throne of God is not done through a physical posture, nor a particular ritual, nor a stay in a sacred place. Instead, it is done by observing the divine commandments that govern it.

It is this invisible yet regulating truth to which the Lord Jesus Christ was alluding through the phrase "worship in truth," mentioned in the preceding declaration.

What are these divine commandments that govern the approach to the throne of God?

What are the mysteries that establish them as the divine commandments governing this approach?

According to what has been revealed to us, these commandments are the first four of the ten that God gave to the prophet Moses on Mount Sinai, which He detailed as follows:

> "You shall have no other gods before me" (Exodus 20:3).
>
> You shall not make for yourself an image in the form of anything in heaven above or on the earth beneath or in the waters below. You shall not bow down to them or worship them; for I, the LORD your God, am a jealous God, punishing the children for the sin of the parents to the third and fourth generation of those who hate me, but showing love to a thousand generations of those who love me and keep my commandments. (Exodus 20:4–6)
>
> "You shall not misuse the name of the LORD your God, for the LORD will not hold anyone guiltless who misuses his name" (Exodus 20:7).

> Remember the Sabbath day by keeping it holy. Six days you shall labor and do all your work, but the seventh day is a sabbath to the LORD your God. On it you shall not do any work, neither you, nor your son or daughter, nor your male or female servant, nor your animals, nor any foreigner residing in your towns. For in six days the LORD made the heavens and the earth, the sea, and all that is in them, but he rested on the seventh day. Therefore the LORD blessed the Sabbath day and made it holy. (Exodus 20:8–11)

Before unveiling the mysteries that establish these first four commandments as the divine commandments governing the approach to the throne of God, it is essential to ask a question to clarify any ambiguity concerning the law to which these commandments belong.

This question is as follows: Is it not written that the Lord Jesus Christ is the end of the law of Moses?

Indeed, it is written: "Christ is the end of the law for righteousness to everyone who believes" (Romans 10:4 ESV).

However, when we examine this verse in the light of the Holy Spirit, we understand that the law of Moses, of which the Lord Jesus Christ is the end, refers to the law of sin offerings and their rituals, called the law of the sin offering (Leviticus 6:24–25 ESV), not to the Ten Commandments, also called the Ten

Words, which constitute the law of the covenant (Exodus 34:28 ESV).

This is explained by the fact that:

- The Lord Jesus Christ is the perfect atoning sacrifice of infinite and eternal value, offering us the eternal redemption of our sins (1 John 2:2; Hebrews 9:12).
- His mission on earth was not to break God's covenant with Israel, but to transform it into an entirely spiritual, individual, and inclusive covenant, in fulfillment of the plan of salvation revealed in Genesis 22:15–18 and Jeremiah 31:31–34, and explained, respectively, in Galatians 3:6–9 and Ephesians 2:11–19.

THE MYSTERIES OF THE FIRST FOUR COMMANDMENTS

Under the new covenant, the mysteries of the first four commandments that establish them as the divine commandments governing the approach to the throne of God lie in the fact that:

1. These first four commandments rebuild, in the heart of a person who observes them, a spiritual altar—invisible yet real—that God has placed in the spirit of every creature capable of addressing Him, called the altar of incense, which we human beings lost because of the sin of Adam and Eve.

2. They make this altar active.

This altar is called by the name of the one who stands before the throne of God (Revelation 9:13) and by the name of the one that the prophet Moses built for the tabernacle (Exodus 30:1–8), because it is the same (Hebrews 8:5).

THE RECONSTRUCTION OF THE ALTAR OF INCENSE IN THE HEART

How do the first four commandments rebuild the altar of incense in the heart of a person who observes them?

Before answering this question, it should be noted that the first four commandments derive from the first and greatest commandment of the law of the covenant:

> "Love the Lord your God with all your heart and with all your soul and with all your mind and with all your strength" (Matthew 22:37 and Deuteronomy 6:5, synthesized, harmonized, and paraphrased, as it has been revealed to us).

To rebuild the altar of incense in the heart of a person who observes them, the first four commandments give rise, within that person, to the four forms of love for God that they imply.

If that person cultivates them, these four forms of love for God rebuild the altar of incense in their heart, for it is they who, spiritually, constitute this altar.

The four sides that give the altar of incense the shape of a quadrangular table, as well as the four horns that protrude from it, as described in Exodus 30:1–3 or beheld in vision in Revelation 9:13, are nothing more than the outward manifestation that these four forms of love for God take when they compose the altar of incense: one side and one horn manifest one form of love for God.

What does it mean to cultivate these four forms of love for God, set forth in the first and greatest commandment of the law of the covenant?

To cultivate these four forms of love for God, set forth in the first and greatest commandment of the law of the covenant, according to divine understanding, does not mean developing and nurturing feelings for God, but rather honoring the commitments that these four forms of love for Him imply.

These commitments are as follows:

- Loving God with all our heart implies committing ourselves to living for Him.
- Loving God with all our soul implies committing ourselves to making His choices our choices.
- Loving God with all our mind implies committing ourselves to giving Him priority in everything we plan and intend to do.
- Loving God with all our strength implies committing ourselves to making our body an instrument for Him and Him alone.

On the scale of spiritual dimensions that stimulate immediate answers to prayer, this altar of incense, thus rebuilt, enables that person to attain the first spiritual dimension.

THE ACTIVATION OF THE ALTAR OF INCENSE

How do the first four commandments make the altar of incense of a person who observes them active?

To make the altar of incense of a person who observes them active, the first four commandments arouse, within that person, the commitments that they imply.

These commitments are as follows:

- Committing to having no other gods before the face of God (first commandment)
- Committing to never making for oneself a carved image or any representation of things that are in heaven above, on the earth below, or in the waters under the earth (second commandment)
- Committing to never bowing down to, worshiping, or serving these representations (second commandment)
- Committing to never taking the name of God in vain (third commandment)

- Committing to solemnly sanctifying, worshiping, exalting, blessing, magnifying, praising, glorifying, and celebrating God for who He is—namely, the Creator of all things—at least once a week (fourth commandment)

If that person honors them, these five commitments make their altar of incense active, for these are the five ingredients that make up the spiritual fragrance of this altar. The five ingredients that the Most High, under the old covenant, physically represented by sweet spices, stacte, onycha, galbanum, and pure frankincense (Exodus 30:34–38 ESV).

On the scale of spiritual dimensions that stimulate immediate answers to prayer, this altar of incense, thus activated, enables that person to attain the second spiritual dimension.

THE SPIRITUAL OPERATIONS OF THE ACTIVE ALTAR OF INCENSE

Once activated, the altar of incense, as established by God, performs two major operations to enable a person in whom it is active to approach the throne of God in spirit.

The first operation: *to initiate the divine institution, "prayer," within that person.*

To do this, the altar of incense requires that the gateway, which, under the new covenant, ensures the link between God and humanity, be present in the heart of that person.

This gateway is the Lord Jesus Christ.

This is why He declared:

> "Very truly I tell you, I am the gate for the sheep" (John 10:7).

> "I am the gate; whoever enters through me will be saved. They will come in and go out, and find pasture" (John 10:9).

> "I am the way and the truth and the life. No one comes to the Father except through me" (John 14:6).

God established the Lord Jesus Christ in this role because of who He is before Him.

Who is the Lord Jesus Christ before God?

Before God, the Lord Jesus Christ, also called the Word of God (Revelation 19:13), is God's Spirit made flesh (John 1:14).

In other words, He is the Most High in His function as the Savior of humanity (Colossians 1:15–17).

This is why the angel, when announcing His birth to the shepherds and revealing to them who He is—namely, the Savior of humanity—added: "Who is Christ the Lord" (Luke 2:11 ESV), to signify that He is God, anointed (that is, chosen) by Himself to save His people from their sins (Matthew 1:21).

This truth also stems from the understanding that when an angel utters the word "Lord," it always refers to the Most High.

This is also why the Lord Jesus Christ:

- bears the title "Lord of Lords" (Revelation 17:14), a title solely attributed to God (Deuteronomy 10:17).
- is worshipped by the angels, the four living creatures, and the twenty-four elders (Revelation 5:8–14), a worship exclusively reserved for God (Revelation 4:8–11; Isaiah 6:1–3).

Before God, the Lord Jesus Christ is the atoning sacrifice that made possible the salvation of humanity and its reconciliation with God (Colossians 1:19–22).

In other words, He is the atoning sacrifice that enabled human beings to obtain individually:

- The forgiveness of all the sins they have committed before God (Romans 3:23–25)
- Free access to the throne of God (Ephesians 2:18)
- Eternal life (John 3:16)

This is why John the Baptist, in revealing Him to humanity, called Him: "The Lamb of God, who takes away the sin of the world!" (John 1:29 ESV).

Before God, the Lord Jesus Christ is the supreme High Priest who offered the said atoning sacrifice, making possible the salvation of humanity and its reconciliation with God.

This is why the Holy Scriptures declare:

> In the same way, Christ did not take on himself the glory of becoming a high priest. But God said to him, "You are my Son; today I have become your Father." And he says in another place, "You are a priest forever, in the order of Melchizedek." (Hebrews 5:5–6)

> Such a high priest truly meets our need—one who is holy, blameless, pure, set apart from sinners, exalted above the heavens. Unlike the other high priests, he does not need to offer sacrifices day after day, first for his own sins, and then for the sins of the people. (Hebrews 7:26–27)

> He went through the greater and more perfect tabernacle that is not made with human hands, that is to say, is not a part of this creation. He did not enter by means of the blood of goats and calves; but he entered the Most Holy Place once for all by his own blood, thus obtaining eternal redemption. (Hebrews 9:11–12)

Before God, the Lord Jesus Christ is the Mediator of the new covenant.

This is why the Holy Scriptures declare:

> "There is one God and one mediator between God and mankind, the man Christ Jesus" (1 Timothy 2:5 EHV).

What must a person in whom the altar of incense is made active do for the Lord Jesus Christ, as the gateway that ensures the link between God and humanity, to be present in their heart?

What such a person must do, according to what has been revealed to us, is:

- Accepting Him as their personal Savior
- Accepting Him as their personal Lord
- Committing to addressing God only in His name

What do these commitments mean for us?

- Accepting the Lord Jesus Christ as our personal Savior means believing that He died for our sins and rose again to guarantee us eternal life (Romans 5:8; 6:23).
- Accepting the Lord Jesus Christ as our personal Lord means entrusting Him with the direction of our lives so that He may be our Guide.
  In other words, it means committing ourselves to obeying His word without questioning it (Luke 6:46; John 10:27; 14:15).
- Committing to addressing God only in His name means

including the expression "in the name of Jesus Christ" in all our prayers to God (Colossians 3:17).

Immediately after the Lord Jesus Christ, as the gateway that ensures the link between God and humanity, is present in the heart of that person, the altar of incense initiates, within that person, the divine institution, "prayer," to restore spiritual communication between that person and the Most High.

However, as long as this altar of incense has not yet completed its second operation within that person, this spiritual communication remains limited solely to the prayer of repentance and all that relates to it.

It is the initiation of this divine institution, "prayer," as well as its active and functional state, that the Most High has always represented by the smoke rising from the said altar of incense and ascending before Him (Revelation 8:3–4).

On the scale of spiritual dimensions that stimulate immediate answers to prayer, the initiation, within that person, of the divine institution, "prayer," by the altar of incense enables them to attain the third spiritual dimension.

Before unveiling the second operation of the altar of incense, it is essential to understand why it is crucial to include the expression "in the name of Jesus Christ" in every prayer to God.

Including this expression in every prayer is not only a way of honoring our commitment to address God in the name of the Lord Jesus Christ, but also an act that enables us to benefit from two mysteries associated with this expression.

The first mystery: *this expression triggers the intercession of the Lord Jesus Christ on our behalf.*

Every time a person in whom the first operation of the altar of incense has been completed utters this expression, the divine institution, "prayer," projects before God the work of the cross of the Lord Jesus Christ, accompanied by the living voice of the Lord Jesus Christ interceding on behalf of that person or on behalf of the individual or individuals for whom that person is addressing God.

This is why the Holy Scriptures declare:

> Who shall bring any charge against God's elect? It is God who justifies. Who is to condemn? Christ Jesus is the one who died—more than that, who was raised—who is at the right hand of God, who indeed is interceding for us. (Romans 8:33–34 ESV)

> "Therefore he is able to save completely those who come to God through him, because he always lives to intercede for them" (Hebrews 7:25).

The second mystery: *this expression triggers the fulfillment of a promise that the Lord Jesus Christ made to us.*

This promise is as follows:

> "I will do whatever you ask in my name so that the Father may be glorified in the Son. If you ask me for anything in my name, I will do it" (John 14:13–14 EHV).

It should be noted that this promise, as established by God, is fulfilled in our lives, as well as in the lives of those for whom we intercede, only within the limits of the spiritual dimension that stimulates immediate answers to prayer we have attained.

The second operation: *to transform that person into a temple of God.*

To initiate this transformation, the altar of incense requires that the atoning blood of the Lord Jesus Christ be applied to its horns.

For this to occur, that person must offer a prayer of repentance to God.

What is a prayer of repentance? According to divine understanding, a prayer of repentance is one in which a person:

- Acknowledges and confesses the sins they have committed before God

- Expresses profound regret for these sins
- Commits to never repeating them
- Asks for forgiveness (Proverbs 28:13; 1 John 1:9)

It should be noted that in the prayer-answering process, a prayer of repentance truly becomes the stimulating element of the second operation of the altar of incense only when it is driven by genuine sincerity and a profound desire for transformation and closeness with God.

Once that person has offered a prayer of repentance to God, God has accepted to forgive them, and the atoning blood of the Lord Jesus Christ—granted by God in response to a prayer of repentance—is applied back to the horns of that person's altar of incense, that person's altar of incense transforms that person into a temple of God.

This transformation into a temple of God is the spiritual state that allows prayer, as a divine institution, to operate within us without restriction as to what it transmits.

It is also the sacred place where God meets with every creature who approaches Him (Exodus 25:22), for this is where He dwells, as confirmed by the Holy Scriptures:

> "However, the Most High does not live in houses made by human hands, just as the prophet says" (Acts 7:48 EHV).

"The God who made the world and everything in it is the Lord of heaven and earth and does not live in temples built by human hands" (Acts 17:24).

"Do you not know that you are God's temple and that God's Spirit dwells in you?" (1 Corinthians 3:16 ESV).

On the scale of spiritual dimensions that stimulate immediate answers to prayer, this transformation into a temple of God, accomplished by the altar of incense, enables that person to attain the fourth spiritual dimension.

THE TRANSFORMATION INTO A TEMPLE OF GOD

What we need to know about the transformation into a temple of God, also called the baptism of the Holy Spirit or the reception of the Holy Spirit (Acts 1:4–5; 2:38), is that:

- It can occur:
  - before, during, or after water baptism in the name of Jesus Christ (Acts 10:44–48; 8:14–17).

  - with or without the laying on of hands by a servant of God (Acts 19:5–6; 2:1–4).

  This is explained by the fact that the transformation into a temple of God depends neither on water baptism nor on the laying on of hands, but solely on the elements required to attain the fourth spiritual dimension that stimulates immediate answers to prayer.

- It is always accompanied by signs.

  Some of these signs serve to confirm to a person transformed into a temple of God that they have approached the throne of God, while others mark their belonging to God.

  Among the signs confirming to a person transformed into a temple of God that they have approached the throne of God, the most common are:

  - Inner lightness.

    It manifests as a profound relief, an inner liberation, as if a heavy burden has been lifted.

    A person transformed into a temple of God feels this lightness, for at the moment of their transformation, Satan and his demons have been cast out from them and all the altars they had erected within them have been destroyed (1 John 3:8; Colossians 1:12–13).

    This expulsion of Satan and his demons, as well as the destruction of their altars, is explained by the fact that in the temple of God, there is only one altar—

the altar of incense—and only the Most High reigns there.

This lightness is usually very intense for a while after the transformation into a temple of God and becomes habitual with time.

- Inner peace.

  Also called the peace of God (Philippians 4:7) or the peace of the Lord Jesus Christ (John 14:27).

  A person transformed into a temple of God continually feels this peace thanks to the presence of God's Spirit within them.

  This peace is explained by the fact that where the Most High dwells, there is always abundant peace.

  This is why He is called the God of peace (1 Thessalonians 5:23) and His only Son, the Prince of Peace (Isaiah 9:6).

Among the signs marking the belonging of a person transformed into a temple of God to God, the most common is the radiance of holiness.

A person transformed into a temple of God continually exudes this radiance of holiness thanks to the luminous rays of holiness that God's Spirit constantly emits within them, enabling them to be holy before God.

The radiance of holiness is what, on a spiritual level, gives a person transformed into a temple of God the appearance of a lamp or torch, for it manifests in the form of a bright light emanating from them.

This is why the Lord Jesus Christ declared:

> "I am the light of the world. Whoever follows me will never walk in darkness, but will have the light of life" (John 8:12).
>
> "You are the light of the world" (Matthew 5:14).

This radiance of holiness is also what gives angels and heavenly creatures their lightning-like appearance, as well as the dazzling whiteness of their garments (Matthew 28:2–3), for they too are temples of God.

Although rare, this radiance of holiness can sometimes physically appear on the body of a person belonging to God, but only for a short time.

Three biblical figures experienced this phenomenon during their earthly lives:

- The Lord Jesus Christ (Matthew 17:1–2)
- The prophet Moses (Exodus 34:29–30)
- The deacon Stephen (Acts 6:15)

Perhaps we are wondering how, under the old covenant and the period preceding it, the first four commandments fulfilled these mysteries that establish them as the divine commandments governing the approach to the throne of God.

Under the old covenant, the first four commandments also fulfilled these mysteries that establish them as the divine commandments governing the approach to the throne of God, yet in a different way.

Instead of rebuilding the altar of incense in the heart of a person who observed them, the first four commandments spiritually linked that person to the altar of incense that stands before the throne of God in the heavenly temple. They did so by associating that person's four forms of love for God with those of the heavenly temple's altar of incense and that person's five ingredients of spiritual fragrance with those of the heavenly temple's altar of incense.

On the scale of spiritual dimensions that stimulate immediate answers to prayer, this association of four forms of love for God with those of the heavenly temple's altar of incense and this association of five ingredients of spiritual fragrance with those of that altar enabled that person to attain, respectively, the first and second spiritual dimensions.

Once the link had been established, the heavenly temple's altar of incense also performed two operations to enable that person to approach the throne of God in spirit.

The first operation: *to initiate a sequence of the divine institution, "prayer," dedicated to that person.*

To do this, the heavenly temple's altar of incense required that the gateway, which, under the old covenant, ensured the link between God and humanity, be present within that person.

This gateway was the genetic heritage of Jacob, whom God named Israel (Genesis 35:10).

To possess this heritage, the only way allowed by God was hereditary. Thus, that person had to be a biological descendant of Jacob.

This is why, under the old covenant, God commanded the children of Israel not to eat blood, which implied not using it for medical purposes (Leviticus 17:14).

This prohibition was based on the fact that God did not want a non-biological descendant of Jacob to receive the genetic heritage of Jacob through a blood transfusion, for during a transfusion, the donor's DNA (deoxyribonucleic acid), although absent in mature red blood cells, is present in the transfused blood, primarily in white blood cells.

Once the genetic heritage of Jacob was detected in that person, the heavenly temple's altar of incense initiated a sequence of the divine institution, "prayer," dedicated to that person to restore spiritual communication between that person and the Most High.

However, as long as this heavenly temple's altar of incense had not yet completed its second operation within that person, this spiritual communication remained limited solely to the prayer of repentance and all that related to it at that time.

On the scale of spiritual dimensions that stimulate immediate answers to prayer, the initiation of a sequence of the divine institution, "prayer," dedicated to that person by the heavenly temple's altar of incense enabled them to attain the third spiritual dimension.

The second operation: *to admit that person into the heavenly sanctuary.*

To initiate this admission, first, the heavenly temple's altar of incense required that the atoning blood be applied to the horns of the earthly temple's altar of incense, which represented it on earth.

This atoning blood was not just any atoning blood, but that of the atonement of all the children of Israel, which remained active for one year on the said horns of the earthly temple's altar of incense, for it was applied there once a year, more precisely on the tenth day of the seventh month (Leviticus 16:29–34).

Second, the heavenly temple's altar of incense required that an atoning sacrifice, offered by that person for the forgiveness of their sins, be burned on the earthly temple's altar of burnt offerings, which represented the heavenly temple's altar of burnt offerings on earth (Leviticus 4:22–35).

However, it is essential to note that this atoning sacrifice truly became the second stimulating element of the second operation of the heavenly temple's altar of incense only when that person's prayer of repentance was driven by pure sincerity and a profound desire for transformation and closeness with God.

The necessity of this atoning sacrifice was due to the fact that, under the old covenant, the altar of burnt offerings—which the work of the cross of the Lord Jesus Christ rendered inactive under the new covenant—was active.

Immediately after the atoning blood, that of the atonement of all the children of Israel, had been confirmed active on the horns of the earthly temple's altar of incense and the atoning sacrifice, offered by that person for the forgiveness of their sins, had been burned on the earthly temple's altar of burnt offering and accepted by God, the heavenly temple's altar of incense admitted that person into the heavenly sanctuary.

How did this admission take place?

First, the heavenly temple's altar of incense transferred rays of holiness—emitted by God and touching it—through the spiritual link that united it to that person.

Second, the heavenly temple's altar of incense caused these rays of holiness to emerge in the spirit of that person, diffusing them as if God's Spirit were present in their heart.

This was intended to produce in that person the effects of transformation into a temple of God and the signs that accompany it without that person being transformed into a temple of God.

This was so because, under this covenant, God's Spirit did not dwell in the hearts of human beings. It was not because God was unwilling, but because human hearts contained sins, for the atoning blood of animals did not remove them, but only covered them (Hebrews 10:1–7).

This is also explained by the fact that God is holy and His nature cannot coexist with sin or share His dwelling place with darkness (2 Corinthians 6:14–16; 1 John 1:5).

In other words, a temple of God is not built upon defiled foundations, but rather through total sanctification, for only total sanctification attracts the presence of God and establishes His dwelling place (Leviticus 11:44–45; 1 Peter 1:15–16).

On the scale of spiritual dimensions that stimulate immediate answers to prayer, this admission into the heavenly sanctuary enabled that person to attain the fourth spiritual dimension.

Before the old covenant—that is, after our world had ceased to be paradise and until the establishment of this divine covenant—the first four commandments did not fulfill within human beings these mysteries that establish them as the divine commandments governing the approach to the throne of God, for the law of the covenant had not yet been revealed to humanity.

To hear the prayers of Israel, His people, or of any human being at that time, God used the means He has always used whenever He wants—on His own initiative—to hear any creature in creation.

This means, which constitutes, in the prayer-answering process, the sole exception to the mysteries of the first four commandments, as well as to the principles they imply, is His omniscience.

Perhaps we are wondering why God established the mysteries of the first four commandments as the standard for being heard by Him, when He can hear us by virtue of His omniscience.

God established the mysteries of the first four commandments as the standard for being heard by Him, because He wanted to give us a means not only to make a covenant with Him, but also to initiate—on our own—communication and communion with Him (Proverbs 28:9; 1 Peter 3:12).

Thus, we can address Him freely, at any time and in any place, without waiting for Him to choose the moment.

THE COMMON POINT OF THE COMMANDMENTS OF THE LAW OF THE COVENANT

In light of what we have just revealed, should we understand that in our quest to approach the throne of God under the new covenant, only the first four commandments of the law of the covenant should be taken into account, while the last six (Exodus 20:12–17), which derive from the second greatest commandment, "love your neighbor as yourself" (Matthew 22:39; Leviticus 19:18), should be neglected?

From the beginning of the process of approaching the throne of God to the stage of being transformed into a temple of God—yes! For the benefit of the last six commandments of the law of the covenant, just as that of the second and greatest commandment, from which they derive, is not to approach the throne of God, but a long and happy life within creation (Deuteronomy 5:16; Ephesians 6:2–3).

However, after the stage of transformation into a temple of God—no! For these two groups of commandments of the law of the covenant, like all the other divine laws and principles, have one point in common: their transgression renders the transgressor unclean before God and deprives them of His presence.

For the first four commandments, this deprivation of God's presence results in a complete break in the relationship between the transgressor and God, for the transgression of the first four commandments or of any one of them, which implies the transgression of the first and greatest commandment of the law of the covenant, destroys the transgressor's altar of incense.

However, for the last six commandments, as for all other divine laws and principles, this deprivation of God's presence results in the loss, for the transgressor, of their state as a temple of God, for the transgression of the last six commandments or of any one of them, just as the transgression of the other divine laws and principles or of any one of them, does not destroy the transgressor's altar of incense, but returns it to its first operation.

It was the same under the old covenant.

The transgression of the first four commandments or of any one of them broke the spiritual link between the transgressing child of Israel and the heavenly temple's altar of incense.

However, the transgression of the last six commandments or of any one of them, just as the transgression of the other divine laws and principles or of any one of them, did not break the spiritual link between the transgressing child of Israel and the heavenly temple's altar of incense, but excluded that child of Israel from the heavenly sanctuary, for the heavenly temple's altar of incense ceased to transfer rays of holiness through the spiritual link that united it to that child of Israel.

THE ALTAR OF INCENSE

What explains its indispensability for approaching the throne of God?

The indispensability of the altar of incense for approaching the throne of God is explained by a spiritual reality that God Himself established, then chose to circumvent in order to concretize His will to dwell among us and within each one of us.

This spiritual reality is that God and we, His creatures—angels, archangels, elders, cherubim, humans, and so on—do not belong to the same spiritual world, but to two distinct and mutually inaccessible spiritual worlds.

- Distinct, for His spiritual world is of infinitely superior existential dimensions (Isaiah 57:15), while ours, although diverse, are of lower existential dimensions. This is what justifies His title "the Most High."
- Mutually inaccessible, for we cannot approach Him in His spiritual world because of His dimensional superiority; and, as He is, He cannot come directly to us, for our spiritual worlds, even reunited, cannot contain Him (2 Chronicles 2:6).

To circumvent this spiritual barrier, God, in His sovereignty and infinite wisdom, decided:

1. To establish a spiritual altar, called the altar of incense, access to which is conditioned on the observance of the first four commandments of His law of the covenant as well as the first and greatest commandment, from which these first four commandments derive.
2. To entrust this altar with two essential missions:

- To administer the divine institution, "prayer."
- To create, between His spiritual world and ours as well as within each of us, a spiritual sanctuary of existential dimensions compatible with both those of His spiritual world and those of our spiritual worlds, called the temple of God or the spiritual world of intermediate existential dimensions.

God considered this solution ideal, for it not only concretized His will to dwell among us and within each of us, but also provided us with a spiritual edifice where we can—collectively and individually—fulfill, in His presence, the purpose for which He created us, namely, to worship and serve Him (Daniel 7:9–10 EHV; Revelation 4:8–11; 5:11–14).

This is what explains the indispensability of the altar of incense for approaching the throne of God.

Perhaps we are wondering why we speak of several spiritual worlds of lower existential dimensions, rather than a single spiritual world of lower existential dimensions.

The reason is that according to the revelation we have received, each species of creature capable of addressing God belongs to a distinct spiritual world, whose lower existential dimensions determine its composition, vocation, capacities, and role in creation.

Thus, we creatures do not belong to a single shared spiritual world, but to several spiritual worlds—diverse, orderly, and adapted—in which each of our species flourishes according to the divine purpose assigned to it.

FASTING

In both the Old and New Testaments, fasting is always mentioned in conjunction with prayer. Even today, it is still practiced in conjunction with prayer.

Does this mean that fasting is an option or a condition in the prayer-answering process?

The answer is no! For in all that has been revealed to us about the prayer-answering process, nowhere is fasting mentioned as an option or a condition.

However, although it is neither an option nor a condition for anything in the prayer-answering process, it has been revealed to us that fasting—if sincere—holds special value before God. God perceives it as a way of humbling oneself before Him.

When perceived in this way, first, fasting becomes a stimulus for God's mercy, for God grants forgiveness only to those who humble themselves before Him (2 Chronicles 7:14 ESV).

The most striking example of this dimension of fasting is that of King Ahab, as reported in the Holy Scriptures:

> There had never been anyone like Ahab, who sold himself to do evil in the eyes of the LORD, incited by

> his wife Jezebel. He committed obscene acts by following filthy idols, like everything that the Amorites had done, for which the LORD drove them out before the people of Israel. But when Ahab heard these words, he cried out and tore his clothes. He put on sackcloth and fasted. He slept in sackcloth and went around in a subdued manner. Then the word of the LORD came to Elijah from Tishbe, saying, "Have you seen how Ahab has humbled himself before me? Because he has humbled himself before me, I will not bring this disaster during his days, but during the days of his son I will bring disaster upon his house." (1 Kings 21:25–29 EHV)

Second, fasting becomes the stimulus for God's grace, for God gives grace to those who humble themselves before Him (James 4:6 ESV; Proverbs 3:34 EHV).

The most striking examples of this dimension of fasting are those of Queen Esther and Mordecai (Esther 4–10).

Thus, fasting—if sincere—becomes a powerful spiritual lever that facilitates our approach to the throne of God and the answering of our prayers.

This truth is explained by the fact that, in our quest to approach the throne of God, His forgiveness remains indispensable for the altar of incense to initiate its second operation within us.

Likewise, in our quest to be answered by God, His interventions in our lives or in the lives of those for whom we intercede are not solely a matter of merit, but also of grace.

What makes fasting sincere before God?

What makes fasting sincere before God is neither the nature of the deprivation nor its duration, but the depth of the intention to humble oneself before God that accompanies it.

For us who aspire to approach the throne of God and be answered by Him, this intention must be profound and genuine. Without this, our fasting would be nothing more than mere abstinence from food, devoid of any spiritual impact.

Chapter 2

THE ANSWERING OF PRAYER

By definition, the answering of prayer is the process by which God responds to prayers that reach His ears.

To respond to these prayers, God uses two divine institutions: the divine messenger and the right hand of the Lord (Psalm 118:16 EHV; Psalm 89:13 EHV).

THE DIVINE MESSENGER

Through the divine institution, "the divine messenger," God responds to all prayers for which His response consists solely of a message.

Here is how He proceeds: When a prayer reaches His ears and His response to that prayer consists solely of a message, God transmits that message to a messenger angel who, in turn, communicates it either directly to its recipient or to a third party mandated to convey it to them.

The most striking examples of prayers answered through this divine institution are those of:

- The prophet Daniel (Daniel 9:20–23; 10:2–12)
- Manoah, the father of Samson (Judges 13:8–24)
- The priest Zechariah (Luke 1:5–25)
- The centurion Cornelius (Acts 10:1–8)

THE RIGHT HAND OF THE LORD

Through the divine institution, "the right hand of the Lord," God responds to all prayers for which His response consists solely of direct intervention.

As for how He proceeds, it has been revealed to us that God proceeds in two ways:

- The way of direct command
- The way of indirect command

THE WAY OF DIRECT COMMAND

When a prayer reaches His ears, His response to that prayer consists solely of direct intervention, and He chooses to proceed with that response by direct command, God issues direct commands to the divine powers of intervention, which constitute the divine institution, "the right hand of the Lord."

These direct commands may be:

- To answer a prayer regardless of the state of the soul of the person offering it.
  God often intervenes in this way when the humility of a person invoking Him is profound and genuine.
  The most striking example of this case is the humility of King Ahab before God, related in 1 Kings 21:25–29, cited previously.
- Not to answer a prayer even if the person offering it deserves to be answered.
  God often intervenes in this way when He decides to preserve the salvation of someone who belongs to Him, for in His love, the salvation of His own is always His absolute priority.
  The most striking example of this case is the apostle Paul, who understood that God's refusal to answer his prayer concerning the thorn in his flesh was intended to preserve his salvation (2 Corinthians 12:7–9).
  God also intervenes in this way when the prayer, having reached His ears, is intended to satisfy passions (James 4:3 ESV).
- To delay the answering of a prayer even if the person offering it deserves to be answered immediately.

God often intervenes in this way when He has a greater purpose and is waiting for the ideal moment to respond, for He is the master of time and circumstances, and the only one who knows the appointed time for all things and what is best for us (Daniel 2:21).

The most striking example of this case is Job, whose prayer for restoration was delayed by God because his trial was part of the divine purpose (Job 38:1–2).

- To answer a prayer even if the person or people who benefit from it do not deserve it.

  God often intervenes in this way to manifest His sovereign grace, for He grants grace and mercy to whom He wills, when He wills, and where He wills (Exodus 33:19).

  The most striking example of this case is the healing of the daughter of the Canaanite woman (Matthew 15:21–28).

- To intervene in a person's life without that person having requested it.

  God often intervenes in this way simply out of compassion, for He is infinitely compassionate and abounding in steadfast love (Psalm 103:8; Lamentations 3:22–23).

  The most striking example of this case is the resurrection of the son of the widow of Nain (Luke 7:11–16).

  God also intervenes in this way, or at the request of a third party, when He decides to reveal the glory of His name and manifest His power so that we may believe in Him and His only Son, the Lord Jesus Christ.

> The most striking example of this case is the resurrection of Lazarus (John 11:1–45).

These direct commands may be other than those listed previously, for God is sovereign in His decisions, as the Holy Scriptures declare:

> "The LORD does whatever pleases him, in the heavens and on the earth, in the seas and all their depths" (Psalm 135:6).

> "He does as he pleases with the powers of heaven and the peoples of the earth. No one can hold back his hand or say to him: 'What have you done?'" (Daniel 4:35).

In the prayer-answering process, the answering of prayer by direct command is the exception.

God instituted it for two principal reasons: to answer every creature according to His divine purposes and to control the answering of all prayers for which His response consists solely of direct intervention.

THE WAY OF INDIRECT COMMAND

When a prayer reaches His ears, His response to that prayer consists solely of direct intervention, and He chooses to proceed with that response by indirect command, God allows the divine powers of intervention to act according to the divine principle that governs the answering of prayer through the divine institution, "the right hand of the Lord."

This divine principle stipulates that a divine power of intervention, independently of other divine powers of intervention and in the absence of direct commands to that effect, must answer every prayer falling within its field of action addressed to God by a person who has attained the fourth spiritual dimension that stimulates immediate answers to prayer, provided that its stimulating elements, established by God, are active in that person.

By choosing to answer a prayer by indirect command, God actually allows a person transformed into a temple of God or admitted into the heavenly sanctuary, who addresses Him and in whom the stimulating elements of the divine powers of intervention are active, to trigger the answer to their prayer themselves. In other words, God authorizes the divine powers of intervention to obey that person.

The most striking example of a prayer answered by indirect command is that of the woman who had a discharge of blood for twelve years.

Here is what the Holy Scriptures report about this answer:

> A certain woman who was there had a discharge of blood for twelve years. She had suffered much under the care of many physicians and had spent all that she

> had. Yet instead of getting better, she grew worse. When she heard what was being said about Jesus, she went up behind him in the crowd and touched his robe. She said, "If I just touch his robe, I will be healed." Immediately her flow of blood stopped, and she felt in her body that she was healed of her affliction. At that moment, Jesus knew that power had gone out from him. He turned around in the crowd and asked, "Who touched my robe?" His disciples said to him, "You see the crowd pressing tightly against you and yet you say, 'Who touched me?'" Nevertheless he kept looking around to see who had done this. The woman was trembling with fear since she knew what had happened to her. She came forward, fell down in front of him, and told him the whole truth. He said to her, "Daughter, your faith has made you well. Go in peace and be healed of your suffering." (Mark 5:25–34 EHV)

In the prayer-answering process, the answering of prayer by indirect command is the standard.

The Most High instituted it for a fundamental reason: to confer upon every creature who is His temple or who is admitted into His heavenly sanctuary the power to become a god (Psalm 82:6; John 10:34)—that is, the power to do the works that He and the Lord Jesus Christ do, and even to do greater works (John 14:12).

It is thanks to the possession of this power that:

- Joshua the son of Nun stopped the sun and the moon (Joshua 10:12–14).
- King David slew the giant Goliath (1 Samuel 17:41–51) and defeated a troop of Amalekites with only four hundred men (1 Samuel 30:10–19).
- Stephen performed great wonders and signs among the people (Acts 6:8).
- The apostle Paul performed extraordinary miracles to the point that handkerchiefs and aprons that touched his body healed the sick and cast out evil spirits (Acts 19:11–12).
- And so on.

What are the stimulating elements of the divine powers of intervention that enable us to possess this power?

How can we activate them within ourselves?

Before answering these questions, let us first talk about the divine powers of intervention.

This will enable us not only to unveil the mysteries surrounding the past, present, and future of these divine powers of intervention in our world, but above all to shed light on specific elements that will help us answer these questions correctly.

For, at the end of this revelation, the greatness of the divine powers of intervention—established by the Most High to act within creation and manifest His power—is unveiled.

THE DIVINE POWERS OF INTERVENTION

First of all, what is a divine power?

A divine power is a spiritual force of infinitely superior existential dimensions that gives beings or elements of intermediate and lower existential dimensions the possibility of being or not being.

Concerning their source and their mission, the divine powers draw their origin from the Most High and are appointed to accomplish His purposes and to manifest His will.

Although they share similar characteristics and properties, the divine powers are distinguished by their capacities for accomplishment.

The existence, perfection, and meticulous organization of everything around us—visible or invisible, infinitely small or large—as well as our own existence and that of spiritual beings and elements invisible to our physical eyes, bear witness to their activities.

As for the number of these divine powers, they are counted by myriads upon myriads.

What is a divine power of intervention?

A divine power of intervention is a spiritual force of infinitely superior existential dimensions entrusted with executing God's direct and indirect commands, relating either to the manifestation of supreme happiness in a world of intermediate or lower existential dimensions or to the control of the beings and elements of that world, all within the limits of its field of action and mission in that world.

By "manifestation of supreme happiness," we mean the satisfaction, within the limits determined by God, of the needs of creatures who belong to Him.

These needs can be expressed in the following forms:

- Prayer
- Declaration
- Thought
- Wish
- Desire
- Action
- Emotion
- Nonverbal communication

The divine powers of intervention were revealed to be useful in our world when God declared: "Let us make man in our image, according to our likeness, and let them have dominion . . . over all the earth" (Genesis 1:26 EHV).

From that declaration until today, these divine powers of intervention have already been introduced into our world twice as part of the prayer-answering process, and the third is yet to come.

When did the first two introductions of these divine powers of intervention take place?

What was the mission of each of them?

When will the third introduction of these divine powers of intervention take place?

What will be its mission?

To answer these questions, let us unveil the mysteries surrounding each of these three introductions of divine powers of intervention into our world.

THE FIRST INTRODUCTION OF DIVINE POWERS OF INTERVENTION INTO OUR WORLD

According to what has been revealed to us, the first introduction of divine powers of intervention into our world took place immediately after its creation, more precisely before Adam, the first human being, was established on earth.

To understand how this first introduction took place, let us interpret Genesis 2:8–17 in clear terms, for this biblical passage depicts—through representations and coded expressions—not only the creation of our world and the establishment of Adam on earth, but also the introduction of divine powers of intervention into our world, as well as other related realities.

All of this, as seen from the heavenly temple.

To do this, we will proceed verse by verse and group of verses by group of verses.

> "The LORD God planted a garden in Eden in the east, and there he put the man whom he had formed" (Genesis 2:8 EHV).

This verse reveals that first, God created a new spiritual world of lower existential dimensions; second, He integrated physical dimensions into it. It is this integration that is expressed by the coded expression "and there he put the man whom he had formed."

God positioned this world to the east of Eden, more precisely to the east of the heavenly temple.

To gain a general understanding of the arrangement of the spiritual worlds, which will enable us to understand the arrangement of our world that we have just revealed, two questions must be asked.

What is Eden?

According to what has been revealed to us, Eden is the heaven (Matthew 23:9)—that is, the kingdom of God.

It is composed of the spiritual world of infinitely superior existential dimensions, the heavenly temple linked to the spiritual world of infinitely superior existential dimensions, and all the different spiritual worlds of lower existential dimensions linked to the heavenly temple.

Why is our world described as a garden in this verse?

Our world is described as a garden in this verse because the way in which the spiritual worlds of the lower existential dimensions are arranged around the heavenly temple gives them the appearance of its gardens.

> Out of the ground the LORD God made every kind of tree grow—trees that are pleasant to look at and

> good for food, including the Tree of Life in the middle of the garden and the Tree of the Knowledge of Good and Evil. (Genesis 2:9 EHV)

This verse reveals two events that followed the positioning of our world to the east of the heavenly temple.

These events are as follows:

1. The link between our world and the heavenly temple.
   After positioning our world to the east of the heavenly temple, God linked it to that temple, thereby enabling human beings to access eternal life.
   This truth is based on the divine principle that in the kingdom of heaven as established by God, the granting of eternal life to the inhabitants of a spiritual world of lower existential dimensions is possible only if that world is linked to the heavenly temple.
   This link is attested by the presence, in that world, of the Tree of Life—an element of the courtyard of the heavenly temple.
2. The granting of free will to human beings.
   After linking our world to the heavenly temple, God, in His sovereignty, granted human beings free will.
   It is this granting of free will that explains the presence of the Tree of Knowledge of Good and Evil in our world, for, in the kingdom of heaven as established by God, the granting of free will to the inhabitants of a spiritual

world of lower existential dimensions is attested by the presence, in that world, of the Tree of the Knowledge of Good and Evil—also an element of the courtyard of the heavenly temple.

What is free will?

According to divine understanding, free will is the capacity to make choices and decisions without external constraint, while fully assuming responsibility for those choices and their consequences before God.

> "A river went out from Eden to water the garden, and from there it divided and became the headwaters of four rivers" (Genesis 2:10 EHV).

The river, which flowed out of Eden, represents the divine institution, "the right hand of the Lord."

Its four branches represent the four divine powers of intervention that constitute this divine institution.

The coded expression "to water the garden" signifies that the four divine powers of intervention were introduced into our world and then integrated into its lower existential dimensions in order to transform it into paradise.

> The name of the first river is Pishon. It flows through the whole land of Havilah, where there is gold, and the gold of that land is good. Incense and onyx stone are also found there. The name of the second river is

> Gihon. It is the same river that winds through the whole land of Cush. The name of the third river is Tigris. This is the one which flows along the east side of Assyria. The fourth river is the Euphrates. (Genesis 2:11–14 EHV)

These verses reveal the human names God gave to the four divine powers of intervention to confirm their integration into the lower existential dimensions of our world.

These names are:

- Pishon for the first divine power of intervention
- Gihon for the second
- Tigris for the third
- Euphrates for the fourth

> "The Lord God took the man and settled him in the Garden of Eden to work it and to take care of it" (Genesis 2:15 EHV).

This verse reveals that after the transformation of our world into paradise, called the garden of Eden, God placed human beings there not only to reside, but also to maintain the presence of the divine powers of intervention and preserve the link between our world and the heavenly temple.

This is what the coded expression "to work it and to take care of it" signifies. It was not a matter of working the ground to make it produce, for in paradise, the four divine powers of intervention provided for all human needs.

Why did God entrust human beings with the responsibility of maintaining the presence of the divine powers of intervention in our world and of preserving the link between our world and the heavenly temple?

God entrusted human beings with this responsibility because they were the primary beneficiaries of supreme happiness and eternal life, which are ensured, respectively, by the divine powers of intervention and the link between our world and the heavenly temple.

> The LORD God gave a command to the man. He said, "You may freely eat from every tree in the garden, but you shall not eat from the Tree of the Knowledge of Good and Evil, for on the day that you eat from it, you will certainly die." (Genesis 2:16–17 EHV)

These verses reveal the stimulating element of the divine powers of intervention that human beings must activate within themselves to maintain supreme happiness and eternal life in our world.

This stimulating element was the command:

> "You shall not eat from the Tree of the Knowledge of Good and Evil."

To activate this stimulating element within themselves, human beings had to obey that command.

When were the divine powers of intervention withdrawn from our world for the first time?

The divine powers of intervention were withdrawn from our world for the first time after human beings had disobeyed the command: "You shall not eat from the Tree of the Knowledge of Good and Evil," more precisely when the Most High had fulfilled in their lives what He meant by the coded expression "on the day you eat of it, you will die."

As for how the Most High fulfilled, in human beings' lives, what He meant by this coded expression, the Holy Scriptures report:

> The LORD God sent him out from the Garden of Eden to work the soil from which he had been taken. So he drove the man out, and in front of the Garden of Eden he stationed cherubim and a flaming sword, which turned in every direction to guard the way to the Tree of Life. (Genesis 3:23–24 EHV)

These verses reveal that God first withdrew the divine powers of intervention from our world. As a result, our world ceased to be paradise, forcing human beings to work the ground to provide for themselves. Then God detached our world from the heavenly temple, causing human beings to lose eternal life.

Even before fulfilling these two acts, God announced to

human beings the trials that awaited them in a world deprived of supreme happiness and eternal life. He expressed this announcement with the following words:

> To the woman he said, "I will surely multiply your pain in childbearing; in pain you shall bring forth children. Your desire shall be for your husband, and he shall rule over you." And to Adam he said, "Because you have listened to the voice of your wife and have eaten of the tree of which I commanded you, 'You shall not eat of it,' cursed is the ground because of you; in pain you shall eat of it all the days of your life; thorns and thistles it shall bring forth for you; and you shall eat the plants of the field. By the sweat of your face you shall eat bread, till you return to the ground, for out of it you were taken; for you are dust, and to dust you shall return." (Genesis 3:16–19 ESV)

With these words, God wanted to make it clear to human beings that they were not created to live independently of Him. When human beings understood this truth, it was already too late—the misfortune announced by God had befallen them.

In despair, human beings then began seeking God, offering Him sacrifices, and calling upon His name (Genesis 4:3–4, 26), hoping that God would grant them grace and lift the divine curse from their world.

However, the responses they received from God—whenever they managed to find Him—were limited to a favorable gaze or to a few recommendations or reproaches (Genesis 4:4–13), for God had left them to their sad fate.

THE SECOND INTRODUCTION OF DIVINE POWERS OF INTERVENTION INTO OUR WORLD

Although it is not detailed in the Holy Scriptures as the first, the second introduction of the divine powers of intervention into our world took place, according to what has been revealed to us, after the birth of Noah, more precisely after his father Lamech uttered over him this prophetic word: "This one will bring us comfort during our work and the hard labor that we must perform with our hands because the LORD has cursed the soil" (Genesis 5:29 EHV).

This prophetic word, which the Most High had placed in Lamech's heart, was not only the prophecy that triggered the second introduction of divine powers of intervention into our world, but also the element that marked the beginning of humanity's salvation calendar and the enthronement of Noah as the first chosen descendant of Enoch's chosen bloodline.

All of this was one of the consequences of the first two of the three decisions God made after being very pleased with the way Enoch, Noah's great-grandfather, walked before Him (Genesis 5:22).

What were these first two decisions God made?

The first decision was to reconcile with humanity.

God made this decision because of Enoch's conduct, which proved to Him that human beings are capable of fearing Him and fulfilling the purposes for which He created them if He grants them a second chance.

In His sovereignty, God decided that this reconciliation would unfold gradually. He initiated this reconciliation:

- First with Enoch, for He had decided to take him into His kingdom of heaven (Genesis 5:24)
- Then with Enoch's chosen bloodline
- Finally, with all of humanity (2 Corinthians 5:18–19; Romans 5:10–11)

The second decision was to establish a people from Enoch's seed—a people that would belong to Him forever, over whom He would reign for eternity, and who would bear the name Israel.

In His sovereignty, God decided that this people would be composed according to the following two aspects of the plan of salvation:

- Physical Israel: all people descended from Enoch's chosen bloodline.
- Spiritual Israel: all people who share Enoch's spiritual quality—namely, the fear of God.

How did God proceed to establish Israel, His people?

God established Israel, His people, by proceeding through four stages spread out over time and ordered according to His wisdom.

First, God chose twelve biological descendants of Enoch—whom we call Enoch's chosen bloodline—among whom:

- Noah the son of Lamech was the first (Genesis 5:28–29).
- Shem the son of Noah, the second (Genesis 5:32).
- Arphaxad the son of Shem, the third (Genesis 11:10–11).
- Shelah the son of Arpachshad, the fourth (Genesis 11:12–13).
- Eber the son of Shelah, the fifth (Genesis 11:14–15).
- Peleg the son of Eber, the sixth (Genesis 11:16–17).
- Reu the son of Peleg, the seventh (Genesis 11:18–19).
- Serug the son of Reu, the eighth (Genesis 11:20–21).
- Nahor the son of Serug, the ninth (Genesis 11:22–23).
- Terah the son of Nahor, the tenth (Genesis 11:24–25).
- Abram the son of Terah—whom He named Abraham—the eleventh (Genesis 11:26; 17:5).
- Isaac the son of Abraham, the twelfth (Genesis 21:1–3 EHV).

Second, God chose Jacob, the son of Isaac, and made him Israel, His people (Romans 9:10–13; Genesis 35:10).

Third, God chose the twelve sons of Jacob:

- Reuben

- Simeon
- Levi
- Judah
- Dan
- Naphtali
- Gad
- Asher
- Issachar
- Zebulun
- Joseph
- Benjamin (Exodus 1:1–5)

He made them the twelve physical and spiritual patriarchs of Israel, His people, although, in the tribal distribution, Levi and Joseph were replaced by Manasseh and Ephraim (Joshua 14:4).

Fourth, after the establishment of the new covenant, God chose:

- Simon, called Peter
- Andrew, the brother of Peter
- James the son of Zebedee
- John the son of Zebedee
- Philip
- Bartholomew
- Matthew
- Thomas
- James the son of Alphaeus

- Thaddaeus, also called Judas, the son of James
- Simon, called the Zealot
- In place of Judas Iscariot—not Matthias, whom the eleven apostles chose by casting lots (Acts 1:21–26)—but Saul of Tarsus, called Paul (Acts 9:11–15)

He made them not only the twelve apostles of the Lord Jesus Christ (Matthew 10:2–4; Luke 6:13–16), but also the twelve spiritual patriarchs of Israel, His people, replacing the twelve sons of Jacob.

As for the composition of the two aspects of Israel:

- Physical Israel includes all the biological descendants of Jacob, also called the children of Israel or Israelites.
- Spiritual Israel, meanwhile, includes all the biological descendants of Jacob who have attained the fourth spiritual dimension that stimulates immediate answers to prayer and all the non-biological descendants of Jacob who have attained this same spiritual dimension.

Each of these two aspects of Israel is part of a divine purpose:

- Physical Israel is the custodian of God's:
  - Laws
  - Covenants
  - Promises
  - Oracles (Romans 9:3–5 EHV; Romans 3:1–2 ESV; Psalms 147:19–20)

- Spiritual Israel, meanwhile, is:
  - The chosen race
  - A royal priesthood
  - The holy nation
  - The kingdom of priests (1 Peter 2:9 ESV, Exodus 19:6 EHV)

Concerning the status of the members of these two aspects of Israel before God:

- All the biological descendants of Jacob are inhabitants of the earth, like all other human beings.
- However, among them and among the non-biological descendants, those who have attained the fourth spiritual dimension that stimulates immediate answers to prayer are recognized before God as:
  - His redeemed (Revelation 5:9–10)
  - His witnesses (Acts 1:8; Isaiah 43:10)
  - His children (John 1:12–13)

This is why the apostle Paul, to whom the Holy Spirit revealed this truth, declared:

> This does not mean that God's word has failed, because not all who are descended from Israel are really Israel, and not all who are descended from Abraham are really his children. On the contrary, "Your line of descent will be traced through Isaac." This means

> that it is not the children of the flesh who are God's children, but it is the children of the promise who are counted as his descendants. (Romans 9:6–8 EHV)

This truth was also revealed to the prophet Zechariah in its entirety, but in symbolic form, through a prophetic vision.

Here is what he recounts:

> Then the angel who was speaking with me returned and woke me up in the same way that a man is awakened from sleep. He said to me, "What do you see?" I said, "Look! Right there, I see a lampstand, made entirely of gold, with a basin on top of it, with seven lamps on it, and there are seven channels leading to the lamps that are on top of it. There are two olive trees beside it, one to the right of the bowl, and one to its left." I asked the angel who was speaking with me, "What are these, my lord?" The angel who was speaking with me answered me, "Don't you know what these are?" I answered, "No, my lord." (Zechariah 4:1–5 EHV)

The prophet Zechariah continues:

> Then I asked him, "What are these two olive trees to the right and left of the lampstand?" I asked him a second time, "What are the two olive branches that are beside the two gold conduits that pour out the

> golden oil?" He said to me, "Don't you know what these are?" I said, "No, my lord." Then he said, "These are the two anointed ones who stand by the Lord of all the earth." (Zechariah 4:11–14 EHV)

Here is what these symbols represent and/or signify:

- The two olive trees, one on the right of the bowl and the other on the left, represent, respectively, the children of Israel (the cultivated olive tree) and the nations (the wild olive tree) (Romans 11:24–25).
- Gold represents holiness.
- The olive branch near the gold conduit on the right side of the bowl represents all the biological descendants of Jacob who have attained the fourth spiritual dimension. The one on the left of the bowl represents all the non-biological descendants of Jacob who have attained this same spiritual dimension.

  This distinction is explained by the fact that these two groups, within their respective peoples, are the only ones who, on the spiritual level, exude the radiance of holiness, represented here by the golden oil flowing from these two olive branches.
- The lamps represent all the biological descendants of Jacob who have attained the fourth spiritual dimension and all the non-biological descendants of Jacob who have attained this same spiritual dimension, for they are the

torches of holiness that God distinguishes in the darkness that covers the earth since our world ceased to be paradise (Philippians 2:15 ESV).

- These lamps are seven in number to represent Enoch, the seventh generation of Adam through Seth (Genesis 5:1–18), and to confirm that the biological descendants of Jacob who have attained the fourth spiritual dimension and the non-biological descendants of Jacob who have attained this same spiritual dimension—whom they represent—are the only ones who share Enoch's spiritual quality.
- The seven-branched lampstand, without gold or lamps, represents the human world in its natural dimension, not yet visited by the redemptive grace of God, as manifested in the old and new covenants, for its seven branches evoke the seven days it took God to complete the creation of the human world (Genesis 2:2).
- The seven-branched lampstand, made entirely of gold and bearing seven lamps, represents the redeemed, justified, and sanctified human world, which the Most High calls Israel, His people—that is, spiritual Israel.
- The bowl on top of the seven-branched lampstand, made entirely of gold, as well as the stem and base of this same lampstand, represent the golden bowl full of the prayers of the saints, which each of the four living creatures and the twenty-four elders held before the Most High in the vision of the apostle John (Revelation 5:8).

- This bowl and the seven-branched lampstand, made entirely of gold and bearing seven lamps—as presented—signify that the biological descendants of Jacob who have attained the fourth spiritual dimension and the non-biological descendants of Jacob who have attained this same spiritual dimension are the only ones whose prayers the Most High hears (Psalm 34:15; Proverbs 15:29).
  In other words, they are the two anointed ones (that is, the chosen ones) of the human world who have the right to approach the throne of the Most High.
  This is what the angel meant when he said, "These are the two anointed ones who stand by the Lord of all the earth."

It is to respond to the prayers of these two chosen ones, as well as those of Jacob and the twelve chosen descendants of Enoch, whose answering requires direct intervention, that the Most High has, for the second time, introduced the divine powers of intervention into our world, this time with a mission of consolation. For being merciful and abounding in steadfast love, He could not abandon His people, to whom He had forgiven iniquity and rebellion, in the human world struck by divine curse without consoling them.

However, since Israel, His people, is composed of human beings who are the origin of this divine curse, He could not remove them from this curse during their sojourn in the human world.

This is explained by the following immutable decree:

> "The LORD is slow to anger, abounding in love and forgiving sin and rebellion. Yet he does not leave the guilty unpunished" (Numbers 14:18).

At the time of this writing, these divine powers of intervention are present in our world. They will be withdrawn from it during the rapture to heaven of the biological descendants of Jacob who have attained the fourth spiritual dimension and the non-biological descendants of Jacob who have attained this same spiritual dimension (1 Thessalonians 4:14–17). For, as we have previously revealed, these divine powers of intervention were introduced into our world for them. It is with them that they will depart from our world.

THE THIRD INTRODUCTION OF DIVINE POWERS OF INTERVENTION INTO OUR WORLD

Before unveiling the mysteries surrounding this third introduction, let us first reveal the third of the three decisions God made after being very pleased with the way Enoch walked before Him—namely, to create a new human world.

Here is what God declared when He revealed this decision to Israel, His people, and all of humanity:

> "See, I will create new heavens and a new earth. The former things will not be remembered, nor will they come to mind" (Isaiah 65:17).

This decision was confirmed by the Lord Jesus Christ when He declared:

> "Truly I tell you, at the renewal of all things, when the Son of Man sits on his glorious throne, you who have followed me will also sit on twelve thrones, judging the twelve tribes of Israel" (Matthew 19:28).

God made this decision for two essential reasons:

- To establish all the biological descendants of Jacob who have attained the fourth spiritual dimension and all the non-biological descendants of Jacob who have attained this same spiritual dimension in a human world that shall endure before Him (Isaiah 66:22).
- To grant eternal life to those biological descendants of Jacob who have attained the fourth spiritual dimension and to those non-biological descendants of Jacob who have attained this same spiritual dimension (Romans 6:23).

These two objectives cannot be realized in the current human world, for the divine principle governing the link between the spiritual worlds of lower existential dimensions and the heavenly temple stipulates that a spiritual world of lower existential dimensions—detached from the heavenly temple due to the corruption and sins of its inhabitants—cannot be linked to it again for those inhabitants to regain eternal life. Instead, it is irrevocably condemned to be consumed by fire (2 Peter 3:7).

It is after the creation of this new human world, more precisely before the establishment, on the new earth, of the biological descendants of Jacob who have attained the fourth spiritual dimension and the non-biological descendants of Jacob who have attained this same spiritual dimension, that the third introduction of the divine powers of intervention into the new human world will take place.

To understand how this third introduction will take place, let us interpret in clear terms the vision that the apostle John recounts in Revelation 21:1–22:7, for this vision depicts—through representations, numbers, and coded expressions—not only the creation of the new human world and the establishment, on the new earth, of the biological descendants of Jacob who have attained the fourth spiritual dimension and the non-biological descendants of Jacob who have attained this same spiritual dimension, but also the introduction of the divine powers of intervention into this world, as well as other related realities.

To do this, we will proceed verse by verse and group of verses by group of verses. In other words, we will enter into this vision step by step, gradually unveiling each symbol and each mystery in order to grasp the full revelation.

> "Then I saw 'a new heaven and a new earth,' for the first heaven and the first earth had passed away, and there was no longer any sea" (Revelation 21:1).

In this verse, God shows the apostle John the creation of the new human world: a new spiritual world of lower existential dimensions, with physical dimensions identical to those of the current human world, but without the sea.

> "I saw the Holy City, the new Jerusalem, coming down out of heaven from God, prepared as a bride beautifully dressed for her husband" (Revelation 21:2).

In this verse, God shows the apostle John, in the form of a Holy City descending from Him, the introduction of the divine powers of intervention into the new human world.

> And I heard a loud voice from the throne saying, "Look! God's dwelling place is now among the people, and he will dwell with them. They will be his people, and God himself will be with them and be their God. 'He will wipe every tear from their eyes. There will be no more death' or mourning or crying or pain, for the old order of things has passed away." (Revelation 21:3–4)

In these verses, God reveals to the apostle John the mission of the divine powers of intervention in this third introduction: to transform the new human world into paradise, the sole place where human beings can live without mourning, crying, and pain.

According to Revelation 21:2, this new paradise will bear the name of the new Jerusalem.

> "He who was seated on the throne said, 'I am making everything new!' Then he said, 'Write this down, for these words are trustworthy and true'" (Revelation 21:5).

In these verses, God confirms to the apostle John that the creation of the new human world and its transformation into paradise will indeed take place.

> He said to me: "It is done. I am the Alpha and the Omega, the Beginning and the End. To the thirsty I will give water without cost from the spring of the water of life. Those who are victorious will inherit all this, and I will be their God and they will be my children. But the cowardly, the unbelieving, the vile, the murderers, the sexually immoral, those who practice magic arts, the idolaters and all liars—they will be consigned to the fiery lake of burning sulfur. This is the second death." (Revelation 21:6–8)

In these verses, God reveals to the apostle John that the gates of the new paradise are open to every human being. However, to enter, one must either be a biological descendant of Jacob who has attained the fourth spiritual dimension or a non-biological descendant of Jacob who has attained this same spiritual dimension, for they are the ones who have overcome sin and are children of God (Galatians 3:26).

> One of the seven angels who had the seven bowls full of the seven last plagues came and said to me, "Come, I will show you the bride, the wife of the Lamb." And he carried me away in the Spirit to a mountain great and high, and showed me the Holy City, Jerusalem, coming down out of heaven from God. It shone with the glory of God, and its brilliance was like that of a very precious jewel, like a jasper, clear as crystal. (Revelation 21:9–11)

In these verses, God spiritually transports the apostle John into the future so that he may witness firsthand the third introduction of divine powers of intervention into the new human world and observe other details that were not included in the vision.

> It had a great, high wall with twelve gates, and with twelve angels at the gates. On the gates were written the names of the twelve tribes of Israel. There were three gates on the east, three on the north, three on the south and three on the west. The wall of the city

> had twelve foundations, and on them were the names of the twelve apostles of the Lamb. The angel who talked with me had a measuring rod of gold to measure the city, its gates and its walls. The city was laid out like a square, as long as it was wide. He measured the city with the rod and found it to be 12,000 stadia in length, and as wide and high as it is long. The angel measured the wall using human measurement, and it was 144 cubits thick. (Revelation 21:12–17)

The elements that the apostle John describes in this biblical passage are the first of these details.

Here is what they represent and/or signify:

- The four walls, which form the wall of the Holy City and give it its square shape, represent the four divine powers of intervention.
  God has represented them in this way because their fields of action cover all the needs of human life.
- The number one hundred forty-four, formed by twelve multiplied by twelve, represents spiritual Israel, for it is the only one of the two aspects of Israel that, in its development, has had as its spiritual patriarchs the twelve sons of Jacob, represented by the first number twelve, and the twelve apostles of the Lord Jesus Christ, represented by the second number twelve.

- This number one hundred forty-four is the measurement of the thickness of the wall to signify that the four divine powers of intervention will be introduced into the new human world exclusively for spiritual Israel.
- The number twelve thousand is formed by twelve multiplied by one thousand.

  The number twelve represents Israel, while the number one thousand represents the thousand generations of God's mercy toward those who love Him and keep His commandments (Exodus 20:5–6).

  Thus, the number twelve thousand represents the biological descendants of Jacob who have attained the fourth spiritual dimension and the non-biological descendants of Jacob who have attained this same spiritual dimension, for they are the ones who love God and keep His commandments. In other words, they are the only ones truly in covenant with God.

  This truth is also expressed by the number one hundred forty-four thousand, which is formed by one hundred forty-four multiplied by one thousand—that is, twelve multiplied by twelve multiplied by one thousand (Revelation 7:2–8).
- This number twelve thousand is the measurement of the Holy City to signify that the biological descendants of Jacob who have attained the fourth spiritual dimension and the non-biological descendants of Jacob who have attained this same spiritual dimension are the only ones

to whom the Most High has reserved the new human world—that is, the new paradise.

What the apostle John describes in Revelation 7:9–17 is precisely this truth.

- The twelve gates represent the twelve tribes of Israel. This is why the name of each tribe is inscribed on them. God has represented these tribes in this way because salvation has entered the human world through Israel (John 4:22).
- The presence of an angel at each of the twelve gates of the Holy City signifies that the Most High Himself will ensure the protection of the new paradise as well as that of its inhabitants.

The elements described by the apostle John in the biblical passages that follow fit into the continuity of these details.

> "The wall was made of jasper, and the city of pure gold, as pure as glass" (Revelation 21:18).

The construction of the four walls of the Holy City in jasper—an element of the human world—signifies that the four divine powers of intervention will be integrated into the lower existential dimensions of the new human world in order to transform it into paradise, which was not the case during the second introduction of these four divine powers of intervention into the current human world.

Gold, as previously revealed, represents holiness.

However, the particularity of this holiness is that it can be interrupted by sin.

The beings possessing this holiness are the biological descendants of Jacob who have attained the fourth spiritual dimension and the non-biological descendants of Jacob who have attained this same spiritual dimension, for the Holy Scriptures declare:

> "Surely there is not a righteous man on earth who does good and never sins" (Ecclesiastes 7:20 ESV).

> "Because all have sinned and fall short of the glory of God and are justified freely by his grace through the redemption that is in Christ Jesus" (Romans 3:23–24 EHV).

In contrast, pure gold, as pure as glass, represents continual holiness—that is, holiness that will never be interrupted by sin.

The beings possessing this holiness are the spiritual beings who inhabit the heavenly temple and the worlds of lower existential dimensions linked to it.

Thus, the coded expression "the city was made of pure gold, as pure as glass" signifies that in the new paradise, continual holiness will be the foundation of life.

> The foundations of the city walls were decorated with every kind of precious stone. The first foundation was jasper, the second sapphire, the third agate,

> the fourth emerald, the fifth onyx, the sixth ruby, the seventh chrysolite, the eighth beryl, the ninth topaz, the tenth turquoise, the eleventh jacinth, and the twelfth amethyst. (Revelation 21:19–20)

To properly interpret these verses, let us first reveal the meaning of the following coded expression, cited previously: "The wall of the city had twelve foundations, and on them were the names of the twelve apostles of the Lamb."

This coded expression signifies that the wall of the Holy City rested on twelve stakes, each placed, as revealed to us, beneath the base of the two pillars forming each gate.

Seen from below, these twelve stakes, adorned with precious stones and bearing the names of the twelve apostles of the Lord Jesus Christ, represent the breastpiece of judgment that the Lord Jesus Christ wore over His heart when He entered the heavenly sanctuary to offer His blood to God as an atoning sacrifice.

This breastpiece of judgment, said to be of the Lord Jesus Christ, in reference to His status as the one and only High Priest of the new covenant, is none other than the breastpiece of judgment of the old covenant (Exodus 28:15–29 ESV), to which the Most High made two fundamental modifications to seal the change of covenant between Him and humanity—namely, the inclusion of the non-biological descendants of Jacob in the process of salvation, which was the prerogative of the biological descendants of Jacob.

The first modification concerned the arrangement of the twelve precious stones on the breastpiece of judgment.

Under the old covenant, these stones were arranged in four rows of three stones each, representing the four divine powers of intervention.

In contrast, under the new covenant, these stones are placed in a square formation, with three stones on each side.

The second modification was the inscription of the names of the twelve apostles of the Lord Jesus Christ on these stones, one name per stone, replacing those of the twelve sons of Jacob.

This modification stems from the divine principle that only the names of the spiritual patriarchs of Israel corresponding to the covenant in force are inscribed on these stones.

This breastpiece of judgment is composed of twelve stakes of the wall of the Holy City to signify that the atonement accomplished by the Lord Jesus Christ for humanity in the heavenly sanctuary is the sole foundation that will ensure the maintenance and perpetuity of the presence of the divine powers of intervention in the new human world.

This means that in the new paradise, even if the biological descendants of Jacob who have attained the fourth spiritual dimension and the non-biological descendants of Jacob who have attained this same spiritual dimension were to sin, God would not withdraw the divine powers of intervention from the new human world, as He did in the old paradise. On the contrary, He will forgive them because of the atonement of the Lord Jesus Christ, which has granted them eternal redemption.

> "The twelve gates were twelve pearls, each gate made of a single pearl. The great street of the city was of gold, as pure as transparent glass" (Revelation 21:21).

The twelve pearls, from which the twelve gates are made, represent the twelve chosen descendants of Enoch—those rare and distinguished human beings who constitute the bloodline from which Israel, both physical and spiritual, is descended.

God has represented them in this way because, even though they did not all fear God as their ancestor Enoch did, they were nevertheless better than their contemporaries in their fear of God.

In other words, they were less corrupt than the rest of humanity.

It is precisely this distinction that earned them a special love from God, as the Holy Scriptures declare:

> Indeed, the heavens and the heaven of heavens, the earth and everything that is on it—these belong to the LORD your God. Still, the LORD attached himself to your fathers, loved them, and he chose their descendants after them (that's you!) from all peoples, as it is today. (Deuteronomy 10:14–15 EHV)

The coded expression "the great street of the city was of gold, as pure as transparent glass" confirms that in the new paradise, continual holiness will indeed be the foundation of life.

> "I did not see a temple in the city, because the Lord God Almighty and the Lamb are its temple" (Revelation 21:22).

The absence of the temple of God in the Holy City is explained by the fact that in the kingdom of heaven, there is only one temple of God—the heavenly temple—and all creatures capable of addressing God, who inhabit it, are themselves His temples.

> "The city does not need the sun or the moon to shine on it, for the glory of God gives it light, and the Lamb is its lamp" (Revelation 21:23).

This verse reveals that the new paradise will remain forever free from sin, unlike the old one.

In other words, the new human world will never be plunged into darkness, as the current human world is, for the instigators of sin—namely, Satan and his demons—will have no access to it.

> The nations will walk by its light, and the kings of the earth will bring their splendor into it. On no day will its gates ever be shut, for there will be no night there. The glory and honor of the nations will be brought into it. (Revelation 21:24–26)

These verses reveal that the gates of the new paradise are open to every human being, regardless of tribe, language, people, or nation.

> "Nothing impure will ever enter it, nor will anyone who does what is shameful or deceitful, but only those whose names are written in the Lamb's book of life" (Revelation 21:27).

This verse reveals that, although the gates of the new paradise are open to every human being, access is reserved only for those who have attained the fourth spiritual dimension that stimulates immediate answers to prayer, for they are the only ones whose names are written in the Lamb's Book of Life.

> "Then the angel showed me the river of the water of life, as clear as crystal, flowing from the throne of God and of the Lamb down the middle of the great street of the city" (Revelation 22:1–2).

The river of the water of life, mentioned in this verse, represents the divine institution, "the right hand of the Lord."

> "On each side of the river stood the tree of life, bearing twelve crops of fruit, yielding its fruit every month. And the leaves of the tree are for the healing of the nations" (Revelation 22:2).

This verse reveals that the new human world will be linked

to the heavenly temple, which implies that God will grant eternal life to the biological descendants of Jacob who have attained the fourth spiritual dimension and to the non-biological descendants of Jacob who have attained this same spiritual dimension. For, as we have previously revealed, the granting of eternal life to the inhabitants of a spiritual world of lower existential dimensions is only possible if that world is linked to the heavenly temple.

This link is attested by the presence, in that world, of the Tree of Life.

> No longer will there be any curse. The throne of God and of the Lamb will be in the city, and his servants will serve him. They will see his face, and his name will be on their foreheads. There will be no more night. They will not need the light of a lamp or the light of the sun, for the Lord God will give them light. And they will reign for ever and ever. The angel said to me, "These words are trustworthy and true. The Lord, the God who inspires the prophets, sent his angel to show his servants the things that must soon take place." "Look, I am coming soon! Blessed is the one who keeps the words of the prophecy written in this scroll." (Revelation 22:3–7)

These verses gather and confirm the previous revelations, while concluding the vision with a firm promise: the imminent fulfillment of God's purpose and eternal bliss for those who keep the words of this prophecy.

Here is the revelation of the mysteries surrounding the past, present, and future of the divine powers of intervention in our world, which has enabled us to shed light on specific elements that will help us correctly answer the question of what are the stimulating elements of the divine powers of intervention that enable us to possess the power to do the works that the Most High and the Lord Jesus Christ do—and even to do greater works—and how we can activate them within ourselves.

These specific elements are as follows:

- The number of divine powers of intervention
- Their human names
- Their current mission in our world
- The number twelve, which recurs prophetically throughout the spiritual unfolding of Israel, as a sacred landmark in the history of salvation:
  - Twelve chosen descendants of Enoch
  - Twelve sons of Jacob
  - Twelve apostles of the Lord Jesus Christ

THE STIMULATING ELEMENTS OF THE DIVINE POWERS OF INTERVENTION

If we have carefully followed the interpretation of the apostle John's vision, which we developed in the previous point, we will notice that there is one detail he observed when God transported him in spirit into the future, the meaning of which we have not yet revealed. This is not an oversight on our part, but a deliberate will to speak of it at this stage in order to present it appropriately.

This detail is the twelve stakes of the wall of the Holy City, adorned with precious stones and placed in a square formation, with three stakes on each side.

Thus, these twelve stakes, adorned with precious stones, represent the twelve stimulating elements of the divine powers of intervention.

Their distribution—three stakes on each of the four sides of the wall of the Holy City—illustrates the distribution of these twelve stimulating elements: three for each divine power of intervention.

It was only at the second introduction of the divine powers of intervention into our world that God increased the number of these stimulating elements to twelve and distributed them in this way (Exodus 28:17–21).

The reason for this change remains known only to Him.

As for the question of what these twelve stimulating elements are and how we can activate them within ourselves to possess the power to do the works that the Most High and the Lord Jesus Christ do—and even to do greater works—it has been revealed to us that these twelve stimulating elements are, in reality, twelve commitments we must honor in order to attain the last four of the eight spiritual dimensions that stimulate immediate answers to prayer, called the four spiritual dimensions that stimulate the actions of the divine powers of intervention.

These twelve commitments are those implied by the last six commandments of the law of the covenant as well as by the other divine laws and principles that God gave to the children of Israel under the old covenant and that the Lord Jesus Christ, under the new covenant, summarized and deepened.

These commitments truly become the stimulants of the divine powers of intervention only when they are honored by a person who has attained the fourth spiritual dimension that stimulates immediate answers to prayer.

This is explained by the fact that the divine powers of intervention, as established by God, can only be stimulated by a person transformed into a temple of God or admitted into the heavenly sanctuary.

The number twelve, which recurs prophetically throughout the spiritual unfolding of Israel, is the sacred code symbolizing these twelve commitments.

What are these twelve commitments?

To answer this question, let us unveil the fundamental principles that govern, in our world and in this period of divine consolation, the action of each divine power of intervention in both the answering of prayer by direct command and the answering of prayer by indirect command.

To do this properly, we will also unveil the field of action of each of these divine powers of intervention and present some biblical examples that illustrate their work.

Since the Most High did not rename these divine powers of intervention either at their second introduction or in the vision of their third, we will refer to them by the human names He gave them at their first introduction.

THE DIVINE POWER OF INTERVENTION: PISCHON

The divine power of intervention, Pischon, is the one whose field of action encompasses success, achievement, and prosperity, as well as all that relates to them.

In our world and in this period of divine consolation, it embodies the divine power of intervention that ensures the materialization of the following divine promises, as well as all that relates to them:

> "The Lord will command the blessing on you in your barns and in all that you undertake. And he will bless you in the land that the Lord your God is giving you" (Deuteronomy 28:8 ESV).

> The Lord will open for you his good storehouse, the heavens, by giving rain for your land in its season and by blessing all the work of your hand. Then you will cause many nations to borrow from you, but you yourself will not borrow. (Deuteronomy 28:12 EHV)

> The LORD your God will make you abundantly prosperous in all the work of your hand, in the fruit of your womb and in the fruit of your cattle and in the fruit of your ground. For the LORD will again take delight in prospering you. (Deuteronomy 30:9 ESV)

In the answering of prayer by direct command, this divine power, Pischon, materializes—without any condition other than the direct command of God—answers to all prayers relating to success, achievement, and prosperity addressed to God by a person designated by Him.

This principle is based on the fact that in the answering of prayer by direct command as established by God, the divine powers of intervention operate only according to the direct commands issued by God and intervene only in the life of a person designated by Him.

By "person designated by God," we mean every person—whether God-fearing or not—whom the Most High, in His sovereignty, chooses to fulfill His purposes on earth.

The first striking example of the materialization by direct command of success, achievement, and prosperity in the life of a person designated by God thanks to this divine power, Pischon, is that of King Solomon (1 Kings 3:5–14).

The Holy Scriptures report: "King Solomon was greater in riches and wisdom than all the other kings of the earth. The whole world sought audience with Solomon to hear the wisdom God had put in his heart" (1 Kings 10:23–24).

The second striking example of the materialization by direct command of success, achievement, and prosperity in the life of a person designated by God thanks to this divine power, Pischon, is that of Joseph.

The Holy Scriptures report:

> From the time that Potiphar made him manager of his household, in charge of everything that he had, the LORD blessed the Egyptian's household for Joseph's sake, and the blessing of the LORD rested on everything that he had, both in the house and in the fields. (Genesis 39:5 EHV)

Furthermore, according to Genesis 41:14–43, Joseph, after interpreting Pharaoh's dreams, was elevated to the position of governor over all the land of Egypt—essentially prime minister—thus becoming a key instrument of divine providence.

In the answering of prayer by indirect command, this divine power, Pischon, also materializes answers to all prayers relating to success, achievement, and prosperity addressed to God—but this time by a person who has attained the fourth spiritual dimension—provided that the latter honors the three commitments that stimulate the divine power, Pischon.

These commitments are as follows:

- Committing to choosing a job or activity that is in accordance with God's principles and laws and does not harm others (Colossians 3:23; 1 Corinthians 10:31–32)

- Committing to not using one's position in this work or activity as a cover for wickedness (1 Peter 2:16), which implies rejecting and condemning oppression, exploitation, and all forms of fraud (Deuteronomy 24:14–15; 25:13–16; Jeremiah 22:13)
- Committing to paying the tithe on all income earned through this work or activity (Malachi 3:10) and to being generous, especially to those in need (Deuteronomy 15:7–11; Matthew 5:42)

On the scale of spiritual dimensions that stimulate immediate answers to prayer, adhering to these commitments enables that person to attain the fifth spiritual dimension.

It should be noted that for a divine power of intervention to trigger its action in the life of a person who has stimulated it, that person must perform the following two acts:

- Address to the Most High, God Almighty, a prayer that corresponds to the field of action of that divine power of intervention
- Firmly believe in the answering of this prayer (Mark 11:24)

The reason why, in the answering of prayer by indirect command, these two acts are indispensable lies in the fact that:

- A divine power of intervention is only activated when a prayer—having reached the ears of God—corresponds to its field of action.
- Faith constitutes the spiritual gateway through which a divine power of intervention enters and acts in the life of a person who has approached the throne of God.

This is why the Holy Scriptures declare: "Without faith it is impossible to please God. Indeed, it is necessary for the one who approaches God to believe that he exists and that he rewards those who seek him" (Hebrews 11:6 EHV).

Concerning faith, we need to know that:

- It is born and grows within us each time we listen to the Word of God (Romans 10:17).
- It manifests as confidence in what we hope for and assurance about what we do not see, both of which are distinct from what is natural, for they belong to a higher spiritual order (Hebrews 11:1).
- It diminishes and dies within us each time we choose not to put into practice the Word of God we have heard (James 2:17).

The first striking example of the materialization by indirect command of success, achievement, and prosperity in the life of a person who has attained the fifth spiritual dimension is that of King David.

The Holy Scriptures report:

> "In everything he did he had great success, because the LORD was with him" (1 Samuel 18:14).

The Holy Scriptures add:

> "He died at a good old age, having enjoyed long life, wealth and honor" (1 Chronicles 29:28).

The second striking example of the materialization by indirect command of success, achievement, and prosperity in the life of a person who has attained the fifth spiritual dimension is that of the prophet Daniel.

The Holy Scriptures report: "Daniel prospered during the reign of Darius and the reign of Cyrus the Persian" (Daniel 6:28 ESV).

The uniqueness of this divine power, Pischon, lies in the fact that when it is stimulated or authorized to intervene in a person's life, it unfolds and increases that person's wisdom and understanding, all within the limits determined by God (Proverbs 9:10).

In other words, where Pischon acts, the light of God penetrates the darkness of ignorance, divine order replaces human confusion, and every work undertaken under its impetus prospers according to heavenly purposes (Proverbs 2:6).

THE DIVINE POWER OF INTERVENTION: GIHON

The divine power of intervention, Gihon, is the one whose field of action encompasses the healing and restoration of the body, soul, and spirit of creatures, as well as all that relates to them.

In our world and in this period of divine consolation, it embodies the divine power of intervention that ensures the materialization of the following divine promises, as well as all that relates to them:

> None of your men or women will be childless, nor will any of your livestock be without young. The LORD will keep you free from every disease. He will not inflict on you the horrible diseases you knew in Egypt, but he will inflict them on all who hate you. (Deuteronomy 7:14–15)

In the answering of prayer by direct command, this divine power, Gihon, materializes—without any condition other than the direct command of God—answers to all prayers relating to the healing and restoration of the body, soul, and spirit addressed to God by a person designated by Him.

The first striking example of healing by direct command ensured by this divine power, Gihon, is that of King Hezekiah (2 Kings 20:1–7).

The second striking example of healing by direct command ensured by this divine power, Gihon, is that of Naaman (2 Kings 5:7–14).

The third striking example of healing by direct command ensured by this divine power, Gihon, whose presence was signaled by the stirring of the water by an angel, is that of the sick people at the pool of Bethesda.

Here is the testimony of Scripture about this sacred scene:

> Near the Sheep Gate in Jerusalem there is a pool, called Bethesda in Aramaic, which has five colonnades. Within these lay a large number of sick people—blind, lame, or paralyzed—who were waiting for the movement of the water. For an angel would go down at certain times into the pool and stir up the water. Whoever stepped in first after the stirring of the water was healed of whatever disease he had. (John 5:2–4 EHV)

During His earthly ministry, the Lord Jesus also used by direct command the divine power, Gihon, to heal and restore the body, soul, and spirit of people designated by Him.

Here are some examples of this use:

- The healing of the man with a shriveled hand in the synagogue (Mark 3:1–5)
- The healing of the paralytic at Bethesda (John 5:5–9)
- The healing of the leper (Mark 1:40–42)
- The resurrection of the son of the widow of Nain (Luke 7:11–17)
- The resurrection of Lazarus (John 11:33–44)

In the answering of prayer by indirect command, this divine power, Gihon, also materializes answers to all prayers relating to healing and restoration of the body, soul, and spirit addressed to God—but this time by a person who has attained the fourth spiritual dimension—provided that the latter honors the three commitments that stimulate the divine power, Gihon.

These commitments are as follows:

- Committing to living with respect and love for others, which implies:
  - Rejecting and condemning all forms of violence (Exodus 20:13)
  - Honoring every person, especially one's parents (Exodus 20:12; Ephesians 6:1–3)
  - Preserving the property of others (Exodus 20:15)
  - Abstaining from harming others to satisfy one's excessive desire to possess (Ephesians 5:3)
  - Rejoicing in what one has without coveting what belongs to others (Exodus 20:17)
- Committing to abstaining from all immoral sexual practices by being faithful and upright in all one's actions and relationships (Exodus 20:14; Proverbs 11:3)
- Committing to treating animals with respect and dignity (Deuteronomy 25:4), which implies:
  - Avoiding cruelty and abuse toward them, as well as immoral or unnatural practices involving them (Proverbs 12:10; Leviticus 18:23)

- Killing only those we want to eat or those who want to eat or harm us (Genesis 9:3)

On the scale of spiritual dimensions that stimulate immediate answers to prayer, adhering to these commitments enables that person to attain the sixth spiritual dimension.

The first striking example of healing by indirect command ensured by this divine power, Gihon, is that of the woman who had a discharge of blood for twelve years, related in Mark 5:25–34, cited previously.

The second striking example of healing by indirect command ensured by this divine power, Gihon, is that of Hannah (1 Samuel 1:1–20).

Since the second introduction of this divine power, Gihon, into our world, its field of action has been extended twice by God: first at the establishment of the old covenant, then at the birth of the Lord Jesus Christ.

During the first extension, God authorized this divine power, Gihon, to ensure the healing and restoration of the body, soul, and spirit of a biological descendant of Jacob who had not yet attained the sixth spiritual dimension—provided that a person who had already attained this spiritual dimension interceded on their behalf.

The first striking example of this case is the resurrection of the son of the widow of Zarephath thanks to the intercession of the prophet Elijah on his behalf (1 Kings 17:17–24).

The second striking example of this case is the resurrection of the son of the Shunammite woman thanks to the intercession of the prophet Elisha on his behalf (2 Kings 4:32–37).

During the second extension, God authorized the divine power, Gihon, to also ensure the healing and restoration of the body, soul, and spirit, this time not only of a biological descendant of Jacob who has not yet attained the sixth spiritual dimension, but also of a non-biological descendant of Jacob in the same situation—provided that a person who has already attained this spiritual dimension intercedes and/or pronounces a declaration on their behalf.

The first striking example of this case is the resurrection of Tabitha (Dorcas) thanks to the intercession and declaration of the apostle Peter on her behalf (Acts 9:36–42).

The second striking example of this case is the healing of the lame man at the temple gate thanks to the declaration of the apostle Peter on his behalf (Acts 3:1–10).

The third striking example of this case is the healing of the lame man in Lystra thanks to the declaration of the apostle Paul on his behalf (Acts 14:8–10).

To this day, this authorization remains fully valid and in force.

In addition to using this divine power, Gihon, to heal and restore the body, soul, and spirit of His creatures, God also uses it to inflict illness on the enemies of those who belong to Him, as well as on those who hate or harm them.

He also uses it against those who belong to Him when they disobey Him, for inflicting sickness is an integral part of the field of action of this divine power, Gihon, although it is not included in the answering of prayer by indirect command.

Here are some striking examples of this divine use:

- The sterility of Abimelech and his house: when Abimelech, King of Gerar, took Sarah, believing her to be Abraham's sister, God struck his house with sterility until Abraham, by God's command, interceded on his behalf (Genesis 20:1–18).
- The plague inflicted on the children of Israel: following the rebellion of Korah, Dathan, and Abiram, God struck His people with a deadly plague until the prophet Moses interceded on their behalf (Numbers 16:41–50).
- The tumors of the Philistines: after they captured the ark of the covenant, God struck them with plagues until they returned it to Israel (1 Samuel 5:1–12).
- The illness of King Joram: for his disobedience, God struck him with an incurable intestinal disease that caused him to suffer until his death (2 Chronicles 21:18–19).

THE DIVINE POWER OF INTERVENTION: TIGRIS

The divine power of intervention, Tigris, is the one whose field of action encompasses protection and deliverance, as well as all that relates to them.

In our world and in this period of divine consolation, it embodies the divine power of intervention that ensures the materialization of the following divine promises, as well as all that relates to them:

> "The Lord will grant that the enemies who rise up against you will be defeated before you. They will come at you from one direction but flee from you in seven" (Deuteronomy 28:7).

> "A thousand may fall at your side, ten thousand at your right hand, but it will not come near you" (Psalm 91:7 ESV).

> "Every weapon formed against you will fail, and you will condemn every tongue that rises up to judge you. This is the heritage of the servants of the Lord. Their righteousness is from me, declares the Lord" (Isaiah 54:17 EHV).

In the answering of prayer by direct command, this divine power, Tigris, materializes—without any condition other than the direct command of God—answers to all prayers relating to protection and deliverance addressed to God by a person designated by Him.

Before presenting examples of the answering of prayers by direct command ensured by this divine power, Tigris, let us first unveil the fundamental conditions that stimulate the action of this divine power in the answering of prayer by indirect command as well as its uniqueness.

Thus, in the answering of prayer by indirect command, this divine power, Tigris, also materializes answers to all prayers relating to protection and deliverance addressed to God—but this time by a person who has attained the fourth spiritual dimension—provided that the latter honors the three commitments that stimulate the divine power, Tigris.

These commitments are as follows:

- Committing to telling the truth and avoiding all forms of lying, which implies never spreading:
  - Slander (Leviticus 19:16)
  - False testimony (Exodus 20:16)
  - False report (Exodus 23:1)
- Committing to never taking revenge or holding a grudge against one's neighbor (Leviticus 19:18), which implies practicing forgiveness and letting go of negative feelings (Mark 11:25–26; Colossians 3:13)
- Committing to promoting peace and reconciliation in one's relationships with others by avoiding conflict and

seeking peaceful solutions (Matthew 5:9, 23–24; Psalm 34:14; Romans 12:18; 14:19; Hebrews 12:14)

On the scale of spiritual dimensions that stimulate immediate answers to prayer, adhering to these commitments enables that person to attain the seventh spiritual dimension.

The uniqueness of this divine power, Tigris, lies in the fact that wherever it intervenes—whether in the answering of prayer by direct or indirect command—there is always the presence of one or more warrior angels.

This is explained by the fact that this divine power, Tigris, as established by God, primarily operates through one or more warrior angels whom it mobilizes as instruments of its action.

It is because of this uniqueness that the Holy Scriptures declare: "The angel of the LORD encamps around those who fear him, and delivers them" (Psalm 34:7 ESV).

The first striking example of deliverance by direct command ensured by this divine power, Tigris, is that of the apostle Peter (Acts 12:1–12).

The second striking example of deliverance by direct command ensured by this divine power, Tigris, is that of King Hezekiah and the city of Jerusalem.

After King Hezekiah's prayer (2 Kings 19:14–19) and God's response (2 Kings 19:20–34), the Holy Scriptures report:

> That night, the angel of the LORD went out and struck down one hundred eighty-five thousand men in the camp of Assyria. When it was time to wake up in the morning, there they were—all the dead bodies! Then Sennacherib king of Assyria broke camp and returned and lived in Nineveh. (2 Kings 19:35–36 EHV)

The most striking example of protection by indirect command ensured by this divine power, Tigris, with the additional intervention by direct command of the divine power, Gihon, is that of the prophet Elisha (2 Kings 6:15–23).

Since the second introduction of this divine power, Tigris, into our world, its field of action has been extended once by God. This extension took place at the birth of the Lord Jesus Christ.

During this extension, God authorized this divine power, Tigris, to confer upon a person designated by Him or upon a person who has attained the seventh spiritual dimension, the power to cast out—in the name of Jesus Christ—Satan and his demons.

The most striking example of the exercise of this power by people designated by the Most High—that is, by the Lord Jesus Christ—is that of the seventy-two disciples.

After completing their mission (Luke 10:1), the Holy Scriptures report:

> The seventy-two returned with joy and said, "Lord, even the demons submit to us in your name." He replied, "I saw Satan fall like lightning from heaven. I have given you authority to trample on snakes and scorpions and to overcome all the power of the enemy; nothing will harm you. However, do not rejoice that the spirits submit to you, but rejoice that your names are written in heaven." (Luke 10:17–20)

The most striking example of the exercise of this power by a person who has attained the seventh spiritual dimension is that of the apostle Paul.

Luke, physician and companion of the apostle Paul, reports:

> Once when we were going to the place of prayer, we were met by a female slave who had a spirit by which she predicted the future. She earned a great deal of money for her owners by fortune-telling. She followed Paul and the rest of us, shouting, "These men are servants of the Most High God, who are telling you the way to be saved." She kept this up for many days. Finally Paul became so annoyed that he turned around and said to the spirit, "In the name of Jesus Christ I command you to come out of her!" At that moment the spirit left her. (Acts 16:16–18)

During His earthly ministry, the Lord Jesus also exercised this power to deliver people who were possessed by demons.

Here are some examples of His exercise of this power:

- The deliverance of the demon-possessed man in the synagogue (Mark 1:21–27)
- The deliverance of the bent-over woman (Luke 13:10–13)
- The deliverance of the demon-possessed man in the region of the Gerasenes (Mark 5:1–13)
- The deliverance of the deaf-mute child (Mark 9:17–27)

To this day, this power to cast out Satan and his demons remains fully valid and active.

THE DIVINE POWER OF INTERVENTION: EUPHRATES

The divine power of intervention, Euphrates, is the one whose field of action encompasses the control of beings and elements belonging to the spiritual worlds of intermediate or lower existential dimensions, as well as all that relates to them.

In our world and in this period of divine consolation, it embodies the divine power of intervention that ensures the materialisation of answers to all prayers relating to the control of beings and natural elements.

In the answering of prayer by direct command, this divine

power, Euphrates, materializes—without any condition other than the direct command of God—answers to all prayers relating to the control of beings and natural elements addressed to God by a person designated by Him.

The first striking example of a prayer addressed to God by people designated by Him and answered by direct command thanks to this divine power, Euphrates, although expressed in the form of grumbling, is that of the children of Israel concerning food (Exodus 16:2–16).

The second striking example of a prayer addressed to God by a person designated by Him and answered by direct command thanks to this divine power, Euphrates, with the additional intervention by direct command of the divine power, Tigris, although expressed in the form of a wish, is that of King Darius on behalf of the prophet Daniel (Daniel 6:16–24).

The third striking example of a prayer addressed to God by a person designated by Him and answered by direct command thanks to this divine power, Euphrates, although expressed in the form of a statement, is that of the prophet Elijah concerning the multiplication of the widow of Zarephath's flour and oil (1 Kings 17:7–16).

The fourth striking example is that of the deep sleep of the guards, the breaking of the chains, and the opening of the door during the deliverance of the apostle Peter, mentioned in the previous point, for the divine power, Euphrates, had also by direct command intervened in this deliverance.

In the answering of prayer by indirect command, this divine

power, Euphrates, also materializes answers to all prayers relating to the control of beings and natural elements addressed to God—but this time by a person who has attained the fourth spiritual dimension—provided that the latter honors the three commitments that stimulate the divine power, Euphrates.

These commitments are as follows:

- Committing to practicing justice without favoritism or discrimination (Leviticus 19:15; Deuteronomy 16:19–20; Proverbs 21:3; Acts 10:34)
- Committing to never desiring or loving the path of sin, nor heeding any counsel that leads to it (Psalms 1:1)
- Committing to delighting in the law of God and meditating on it day and night (Psalms 1:2), which implies:
  - Having a positive and devoted attitude toward divine laws and principles
  - Viewing them not as constraints, but as loving guides
  - Taking profound joy in meditating on them and putting them into practice

---

On the scale of spiritual dimensions that stimulate immediate answers to prayer, adhering to these commitments enables that person to attain the eighth spiritual dimension.

The first striking example of a prayer addressed to God by a person who has attained the eighth spiritual dimension and answered by indirect command is that of Joshua concerning the stopping of the sun and the moon (Joshua 10:12–14).

The second striking example of a prayer addressed to God by people who have attained the eighth spiritual dimension and answered by indirect command, with the additional intervention by indirect command of the divine power, Tigris, although expressed in the form of a statement, is that of Shadrach, Meshach, and Abednego concerning their refusal to bow down before the statue erected by King Nebuchadnezzar (Daniel 3:14–28).

The third striking example of a prayer addressed to God by a person who has attained the eighth spiritual dimension and answered by indirect command is that of the prophet Elijah on Mount Carmel regarding fire (1 Kings 18:22–39).

The fourth striking example of a prayer addressed to God by a person who has attained the eighth spiritual dimension and answered by indirect command is that of the prophet Elijah concerning rain, after three and a half years marked by a severe drought triggered by him (1 Kings 17:1; 18:41–45).

The uniqueness of this divine power, Euphrates, in the life of a person designated by God or who has stimulated it, is that it is not limited to answering their prayers: it also confers upon them the permanent power to control beings and natural elements, all within the limits of the ministry entrusted to them.

The first striking example of a person to whom this power was granted as part of his ministry is that of the prophet Moses, who remarkably exercised this power through the following events:

- The transformation of the staff into a snake:
  - The first time: God demonstrated to the prophet Moses that He had granted him as part of his ministry this permanent power to control beings and natural elements (Exodus 4:2–4).
  - The second time: this action served to prove to Pharaoh the divine power (Exodus 7:10–12).
- The following seven of the ten plagues of Egypt:
  - Water turned into blood, the first plague (Exodus 7:17–21).
  - Frogs, the second plague (Exodus 8:1–6).
  - Gnats, the third plague (Exodus 8:16–17).
  - Flies, the fourth plague (Exodus 8:20–24).
  - The hail, the seventh plague (Exodus 9:17–26).
  - The locusts, the eighth plague (Exodus 10:12–15).
  - Darkness, the ninth plague (Exodus 10:21–23).

  Note:
  - The fifth plague (death of livestock [Exodus 9:2–6]) and the sixth plague (festering boils [Exodus 9:8–11]) were accomplished by the divine power, Gihon.
  - The tenth plague (death of the firstborn Egyptians [Exodus 12:29–30]) was accomplished by the divine power, Tigris.
- The division of the Red Sea (Exodus 14:21–22).

- The purification of the bitter water at Marah (Exodus 15:22–25).
- Bringing water out of a rock:
  - The first time at Horeb (Exodus 17:5–6).
  - The second time at Meribah (Numbers 20:7–13).
- The swallowing of Korah, Dathan, and Abiram, along with their households and possessions (Numbers 16:28–33).

The second striking example of a person to whom this power was granted as part of his ministry is that of the prophet Elisha, who exercised this power through a series of remarkable miracles.

- He struck the Jordan with Elijah's cloak and the water was divided, enabling him to cross (2 Kings 2:14).
- He multiplied a widow's oil so that she could pay her debts (2 Kings 4:1–7).
- He turned a pot of poisoned food into an edible meal (2 Kings 4:38–41).
- He made an ax head that had fallen into the water float (2 Kings 6:1–7).

The third striking example of a person to whom this power was granted as part of his ministry is that of the prophet Elijah, who exercised this power through a series of supernatural interventions, demonstrating that heavenly authority can manifest through acts of judgment, control of the elements, and miraculous crossing.

- He called down fire from heaven to destroy two groups of soldiers sent by King Ahaziah (2 Kings 1:9–12).
- He struck the Jordan with his cloak and the water was divided, enabling him and Elisha, his servant and disciple at the time, to cross (2 Kings 2:8).

To this day, this uniqueness of the divine power, Euphrates, remains fully active. One need only be invested in a ministry that requires its exercise to benefit from it.

In addition to answering prayers through this divine power, Euphrates, the Most High also uses it to fulfill His purposes on earth.

Here are some striking examples of this divine use:

- The entry of animals, both male and female, according to their kind, into Noah's ark (Genesis 7:13–16)
- The unleashing of the flood upon the earth (Genesis 7:10–12, 17–24)
- The receding of the waters after the flood (Genesis 8:1–3)
- The confusion of languages at Babel (Genesis 11:1–9)
- The destruction of Sodom and Gomorrah (Genesis 19:24–25)
- The transformation of Lot's wife into a pillar of salt (Genesis 19:26)

- The sending of venomous snakes to punish the rebellion of the children of Israel (Numbers 21:6–9)
- The sending of ravens to feed the prophet Elijah (1 Kings 17:2–6)
- The sending of a great fish to swallow Jonah and vomit him onto dry land (Jonah 1:17; 2:10)

During His earthly ministry, the Lord Jesus also used this divine power, Euphrates, through the following events:

- The calming of the storm (Mark 4:35–41)
- The multiplication of the loaves and fishes (Matthew 14:13–21; 15:32–38)
- Walking on water (Matthew 14:22–33)
- The miraculous catch of fish (John 21:2–8)

Here are the fundamental principles that govern, in our world and in this period of divine consolation, the action of each divine power of intervention in both the answering of prayer by direct command and the answering of prayer by indirect command.

It is within these principles that the twelve commitments have been unveiled—commitments which, when faithfully honored, confer upon us the power to do the works that the Most High and the Lord Jesus do, and even to do greater works.

Perhaps we are wondering how, before the establishment of the old covenant, God responded to the prayers that reached His ears.

After our world had ceased to be paradise and until the establishment of the old covenant, God responded to prayers according to a heavenly logic adapted to each of the two eras that constituted this pivotal period.

In the first era, which spans from the withdrawal of the divine powers of intervention from our world to their reintroduction, God answered prayers with a simple favorable or unfavorable gaze (Genesis 4:4–5).

However, for prayers requiring more extensive intervention, He used the divine institution, "the divine messenger" (Genesis 4:9–13).

This mode of answering prayers is explained by the absence, during this era, of the divine powers of intervention in our world, combined with the fact that the law of the covenant had not yet been revealed to humanity.

In the second era, which spans from the reintroduction of the divine powers of intervention into our world to the establishment of the old covenant, the Most High answered prayers primarily through the divine institution, "the divine messenger" (Genesis 21:17–18).

However, for prayers requiring direct intervention, He proceeded by direct command through the divine institution, "the right hand of the Lord" (Genesis 21:19; 25:21).

This mode of answering prayers is explained by the presence, during this era, of the divine powers of intervention in our world, combined with the fact that the law of the covenant had not yet been revealed to humanity.

THE INSEPARABILITY OF THE DIVINE POWERS OF INTERVENTION

What we need to know about the divine powers of intervention, also called the fingers of God (Luke 11:20; Exodus 8:19), is that, although they are independent of one another, none of them can be stimulated in the life of a person who has attained the fourth spiritual dimension that stimulates immediate answers to prayer without the others being stimulated as well.

Likewise, none of them can be lost in the life of a person who has attained the fourth spiritual dimension that stimulates immediate answers to prayer without the others being lost as well.

This is explained by the fact that the twelve commitments that stimulate these divine powers of intervention, as established by God, cannot be honored partially. They must all be honored after the transformation into a temple of God or admission into the heavenly sanctuary. Otherwise, the person transformed into a temple of God or admitted into the heavenly sanctuary will lose their state as a temple of God or as one admitted into the heavenly sanctuary.

In other words, that person's altar of incense will be brought back to its first operation, for, as we revealed previously, these twelve commitments are those implied by the last six commandments of the law of the covenant as well as by the other divine laws and principles.

Failing to honor them or to honor any one of them amounts to transgressing these last six commandments as well as these other divine laws and principles, which results in the deprivation of God's presence, with all the consequences that this entails in the prayer-answering process.

Here is the full revelation about the hidden mysteries of the prayer-answering process.

Chapter 3

CALL TO SHARING AND COMMITMENT

Let us not keep this revelation to ourselves—let us share it with those around us—for by doing so, not only will we greatly help others understand what they must be and what they must do to accomplish mighty deeds with God, but we will also contribute to winning souls for the Lord (Luke 19:10; Matthew 28:18–20).

May the peace of the Lord Jesus Christ be with us all. Amen!

ABOUT THE AUTHOR

Bovic Tshiamala is a passionate preacher of the Word of God and a devoted worship leader, bringing a message of hope and faith through his ministry.

He serves at the church "Jésus le Bon Berger" (Jesus the Good Shepherd), where he dedicates his time to sharing the gospel and inspiring fellow believers.

Bovic lives with his family in Dallas-Fort Worth, Texas.

To learn more about his ministry or to view memorable moments of his family life, please connect with him on Facebook: @BovicTshiamala.

www.ingramcontent.com/pod-product-compliance
Lightning Source LLC
LaVergne TN
LVHW010840120826
845149LV00017B/3324

* 9 7 8 1 9 7 1 1 2 1 0 1 7 *